Supply Chain Risk Management

Supply Chain Risk Management

Tools for Analysis

Second Edition

David L. Olson

Supply Chain Risk Management: Tools for Analysis, Second Edition
Copyright © Business Expert Press, LLC, 2014.

First published in 2011 by
Business Expert Press, LLC
222 East 46th Street, New York, NY 10017
www.businessexpertpress.com

ISBN-13: 978-1-63157-057-5 (paperback)
ISBN-13: 978-1-63157-058-2 (e-book)

Business Expert Press Supply and Operations Management Collection

Collection ISSN: 2156-8189 (print)
Collection ISSN: 2156-8200 (electronic)

Cover and interior design by Exeter Premedia Services Private Ltd., Chennai, India

First edition: 2011
Second edition: 2014

10 9 8 7 6 5 4 3 2 1

Printed in the United States of America.

Abstract

The supply chain management field is one of the fastest growing fields in our economy, given the heavy growth in international trade as a means to access outsourced production opportunities to lower costs and the growth in information technology to coordinate supply chains. However, this opportunity to lower costs entails significant risks, such as tsunamis, earthquakes, political unrest, and economic turbulence. This book discusses risks in supply chain management, followed by graphic and quantitative tools (risk matrices, selection methods, risk simulation modeling, linear programming, and business scorecard analysis) to help manage these risks.

Keywords

Supply chain, risk management, risk matrix, system selection, Monte Carlo simulation, optimization model, balanced scorecard

Contents

Chapter 1   Introduction 1

Chapter 2   Supply Chain Risk Management Process 11

Chapter 3   Risk Matrices in Supply Chain
Risk Management...29

Chapter 4   Supply Chain Selection Decisions................................43

Chapter 5   Simulation of Supply Chain Risk................................61

Chapter 6   Supply Chain Management Risk Models.......................77

Chapter 7   Optimization Models in Supply Chain
Risk Management...89

Chapter 8   Balanced Scorecard in Supply Chain
Management 111

Epilogue: Recapitulation 125

Notes.. 127

References 131

Index 137

CHAPTER 1

Introduction

Supply Chains and Risk

Supply chains have connected sources of goods to customers for as long as humans have done business. Military organizations have always been involved in logistics, which is moving things over a supply chain, and they still are, as demonstrated by the movement of U.S. and allied forces to Iraq and Afghanistan. But armies aren't the only organizations involved in supply chains. Toyota's lean manufacturing, Dell's make-to-order operations, and Walmart's revolutionary retail operations all rely on supply chains linked across many source organizations through computer systems.

Supply chains provide all of us with many benefits as consumers. Producers of goods and services need to take advantage of the many opportunities for efficiency provided by global linkage. However, these opportunities are not free—they involve risks. This book is about the risks involved in supply chains, especially in contemporary global operations.

Some supply chains can be quite simple—bananas picked in Costa Rica may be directly delivered to the plantation owner who might be living in the Cayman Islands. Beans can be picked in California and delivered to a farmers' market in Nevada. However, most goods require a lot of processing, especially foods and drugs, partially for reasons of preservation and partially for reasons of safety. Standard Oil had a widespread supply chain from oil wells throughout the world to places where crude oil was refined. Steel producers had even more complicated supply chains, from various kinds of mines (again, worldwide) to various processing facilities, to blast furnaces, to open-hearth steel producing ovens, to rolling mills, and on to steel yards, which in turn fed many different manufacturers (shipyards, automobile plants, appliance makers, roller bearing producers, etc.).

It might clarify the definition to describe what is not a supply chain. Different people will define supply chains in different ways, but distance and proprietary relationships can matter. In-plant transportation is not a supply chain. You might think that the involvement of multiple owners matters. However, a supply chain is not defined by multiple owners, as organizations like Standard Oil, U.S. Steel, and Alcoa have had massive vertical global supply chains.

At the personal level, dealing with a headache could conceivably involve picking medicinal herbs from your own garden. That would not involve a supply chain. Most of us prefer the reliability and security of going to a reputable store and purchasing aspirin. Packaged aspirin involves a complex supply chain. It is becoming harder and harder as time passes to think of things that do not involve supply chains. When older people (e.g., the author) grew up, food came from the family farm—not a supply chain. Now there are far fewer people growing up on farms— most people grow up in cities, where food supply chains are necessary.

Globalization and Supply Chain Risk

Supply chains are attractive because they allow access to the most cost-effective sources in a system. Globalization has played a major role in expanding the opportunities for many manufacturers, retailers, and other business organizations to be more efficient. The trade-off has always been the cost of transportation, as well as the added risk of globalizing.

Nearly 1,000 years ago, one of the more interesting supply chains was developed by people living along the Baltic Sea. Trade in the Baltic and North Seas developed in the 9th through 11th centuries. However, the lucrative trading was constantly disrupted by robbers (including Vikings). To protect traders from pirates and to provide safe havens for merchants in their trading posts, the Hanseatic League was formed. This was an early form of supply chain risk management.

Supply chains have always involved risk. The Silk Road connected Europe and China, and its camel caravans were highly vulnerable. One way to avoid bandits was to go by water, and shipping is still a primary means of moving material over supply chains. However, just going over water does not avoid criminal activity, as piracy is nearly as old as the trade it preys upon. Historically, most pirates have operated on the cusp between sanctioned legality and hanging offense. Sir Francis Drake was subscribed (a word for partially funded) by Queen Elizabeth I, who took the attitude that if Drake was successful, he had to turn over half his profits to the crown, while if he was caught, she would support his hanging. Drake got his start by preying on the supply chain between Spain and Latin America. The Spanish would export trouble, tyranny, and disease in return for gold and silver, enabling them to become very wealthy without having to develop much productive capacity. They would instead trade their heavy surplus of gold and silver to the rest of Europe for whatever they wanted (thus providing the demand for wool and food production in England, France, and Germany).

We think of piracy as occurring in the time of Blackbeard and Captain Kidd. But piracy is still very much with us. Pirate attacks have quadrupled in the past 10 years.[1] Hotbeds of piracy today are, of course, off the coast of Somalia, but there has long been a problem in northern Indonesia, and the Caribbean has a strong drug-related supply chain industry. The world's navies are giving more attention to controlling piracy, especially in the area around the Straits of Hormuz, which is important to the petroleum supply chain. Table 1.1 shows some of the estimated costs of providing security to shipping.

Table 1.1. Increased Annual Costs of Security per Ship

Security category	Annual increased cost per ship ($)
Ship-to-shore communication equipment	735.80
Training and hiring personnel	710.40
Security equipment	304.40
Marking ship for global identification	21.60

Source: Adapted from Nankivell (2004).

Piracy is still a major form of supply chain risk. However, there are many other serious threats to supply chains. Severe acute respiratory syndrome (SARS) and bird flu have disrupted travel, as well as shipping. Volcano eruptions have led to supply chain disruptions. The Northridge earthquake in Southern California led to mild disruption of economic activity in that area in 1994. There was a similar impact from the Kobe, Japan, earthquake in 1995. The Sichuan earthquake in China in 2008 had a catastrophic impact in terms of lives lost, but supply chain disruption was temporary.[2] More recently, the disruptions appear to be worse. Earthquakes can lead to tsunamis, which can have a drastic impact on supply chains, especially because the technologically advanced Orient sits on the Pacific "ring of fire."

In 2010 the Eyjafjallajökull volcano in Iceland shut down transportation across most of Europe. Many Europeans got to spend a full week waiting for some means to travel across Europe. Supply chains were also disrupted, as transportation (logistics) is key to linking production facilities in supply chains. Many in Europe found their supermarkets short of fresh fruit and flowers.[3] Supply chains often depend on optimized lean manufacturing, requiring just-in-time delivery of components. These systems are optimized, which means the elimination of slack to cover contingencies such as volcanic disruption of air flights.[4] *Bloomberg Businessweek*[5] estimated the economic impact of Eyjafjallajökull to be in the billions of dollars and cited the need for supply chain flexibility through multiple sourcing, flexible manufacturing strategies, and logistics networks capable of alternative routing.

On March 11, 2011, an earthquake north of Tokyo led to a catastrophic tsunami that destroyed most of a rich area of advanced technology manufacturing. It also severely damaged a nuclear power plant, which at the time of writing was still working on damage control efforts. While the worst impact was in terms of Japanese lives, there was also a major impact on many of the world's supply chains. Organizations such as Samsung, Ford Motor Company, and Boeing found production disrupted because of a lack of key components from Japan.[6] Japanese plants produce about 20% of the semiconductors used worldwide, and double that for electronic components. Toshiba produced one-quarter of the nano flash chips used. On March 14, 2011, Toshiba had to halt operations because of power outages.

Modern supply chains need to develop ways to work around any kind of disruption. What nature does not do to us will be done by our fellow man. Wars, of course, lead to major disruptions in supply chains. Tariff regulations can have an impact as well. In 2002, Honda Motors spent $3,000 per ton to airlift carbon sheet steel to the United States after tariff-related supply disruptions. In January 2011, Volkswagen's, Porsche's, and BMW's supply chains in Germany were taxed by surging demand.[7] Volkswagen had to halt production because of engine and other parts shortages. This was not due to natural disaster or war, or any other negative factor, but rather to booming demand in China and the United States. Lean manufacturing and modern consumer retailing operations require maintenance of supply.

Supply chains can offer great value to us as consumers. Competition has led to better products at lower cost, enabled by shipping (by land and air, as well as sea) over supply chains. Outsourcing allows producers to access the best materials and process them at the lowest cost. Lean manufacturing enables cost efficiency as well. However, both of these valuable trends lead to greater supply chain exposure. There is a need to gain flexibility, which can be obtained in a number of ways:[8]

- Use of diversified sources to enable the use of alternatives in quick response to disruptions
- Flexible manufacturing strategies allowing options to produce critical products in multiple locations with rapid changeover capability
- Flexible product design to reduce complexity and leverage common platforms and parts, thus reducing exposure to supply disruption
- Global logistics networks to access low cost and low risk through multiple routes and contingency shipping plans

Economically efficient supply chains push the trade-off between cost and risk. The lowest-cost alternative usually is vulnerable to some kind of disruption. Some of the economic benefit from low cost has to be invested in means to enable flexible coping with disruption.

Unexpected Consequences

There are many unexpected consequences of taking almost any kind of action. For instance, the cost of obtaining crude oil from Libya might involve the lowest cost for a Spanish refiner. However, along with that low cost comes some risk of political instability. There might be less likelihood of governmental confiscation in Nigeria than in Libya. But conversely, there might be more problems with local crime in Nigeria that eat up the savings expected. So the refiner might consider Venezuela as a source of crude oil. Then the problem of political instability again arises. So the refiner might return to Libya, only to find that war has broken out, eliminating all cost advantages of that source. Supply chains seek long-term relationships. Real life involves many short-term disruptions. We have discussed political disruptions, but nature has the ability to disrupt much more spectacularly than politics.

Supply chains involve many risks, which can be categorized as internal (involving issues such as capacity variations, regulations, information delays, and organizational factors) and external (market prices, actions of competitors, manufacturing yield and costs, supplier quality, and political issues).[9] Specific supply chain risks considered by various studies are given in Table 1.2.

In Table 1.2, examples of internal failures are not widely publicized, although they certainly exist. Supply chain organizations need to worry about risks from every direction. In any business, opportunities arise from the ability of that organization to deal with risks. Most natural risks are dealt with either through diversification and redundancy or through insurance, both of which have inherent costs. As with any business decision, the organization needs to make a decision considering all the trade-offs. Traditionally this has involved the factors of costs and benefits. Society is more and more moving toward complex decision-making domains requiring consideration of ecological factors as well as factors of social equity.

Dealing with external risks involves more opportunities to control risk sources. Some supply chains in the past have had some influence on political systems. Arms firms, like that of Alfred Nobel, come to mind, as well as petroleum businesses. While most supply chain entities are not expected to be able to control political risks, including wars and regulations, they do have the ability to create environments leading to labor unrest. Supply chain organizations have even greater expected influence over economic factors. While they are not expected to be able to control exchange rates, the benefit of monopolies or cartels is their ability to influence price. Business organizations also are responsible for developing technologies that provide competitive advantage and for developing product portfolios in dynamic markets with product life cycles. The risks arise from competitors' abilities in never-ending competition.

Table 1.2. Supply Chain Risk Categories

Category	Risk	Examples
External		
Nature	Natural disaster: flood, earthquake	China 2010; Japan 2011
	Plant fire	
	Diseases, epidemics	SARS
Political system	War, terrorism	Iraq 1991; Iraq 2002; Libya 2011
	Labor disputes	Europe ongoing
	Customs and regulations	United States, Japan ongoing
Internal		
Available capacity	Capacity cost	
	Financial capacity/insurance	
	Ability to increase production	
	Structural capacity	
	Supplier bankruptcy	
Internal operation	Forecast inaccuracy	
	Safety (worker accidents)	
	Bullwhip effect	
	Agility/flexibility	
	Holding cost/order fulfillment trade-off	
	On-time delivery	
	Quality	
	Regulatory compliance	Product safety recalls
Information system	Information system breakdown	Computer system crashes
	Distorted information	
	Integration	
	Viruses/bugs/hackers	

Internal risk management is more directly the responsibility of the supply chain organization and its participants. Business organizations are responsible for managing their financial, production, and structural capacities. They are responsible for programs that provide adequate workplace safety, which has proven to be cost-beneficial to organizations, as well as fulfilling social responsibilities. Within supply chains, there is the need to coordinate activities with vendors and to some degree with customers (through bar-code cash register information that provides an instantaneous indication of demand). Information systems technology provides effective tools to keep on top of supply chain information exchange. Another factor of great importance is the responsibility of supply chain core organizations to manage risks inherent in the trade-off between wider participation made possible through Internet connections (providing a larger set of potential suppliers, leading to lower costs) with the reliability provided by long-term relationships with a smaller set of suppliers that have proven to be reliable.

Conclusion

This short book presents some methods available to support risk management in supply chain operations. It does not pretend to be exhaustive, but it does try to focus on the supply chain decision process and methods to support key typical decisions.

The process of risk management can be supported by planning tools to identify what might go wrong, and by methods to monitor organizational performance. Chapter 2 presents a view of the overall risk management process in supply chains. Chapter 3 presents risk matrices, which have been used in a variety of contexts to identify the riskiest situations that might arise. Chapters 4 through 7 demonstrate the use of models to aid key supply chain decisions. Selection is important in many managerial domains. In supply chains, key decisions include source selection as well as channel or routing selection. Risk is often present in a probabilistic form, so Monte Carlo simulation can be a valuable decision support tool for many supply chain decisions. Chapter 4 presents the SMART technique to aid selection decisions. Chapters 5 and 6 discuss simulation models useful in supply chain management. Chapter 7 presents a deterministic optimization model for channel or route selection.

Chapter 8 discusses balanced scorecards as tools that can be used to monitor key performance indicators within organizations in the context of risk management.

These chapters are short and only give a flavor for the types of models that can aid supply chain risk management. But it is hoped that they demonstrate valuable tools for this important managerial environment in our ever more dynamic and complex world.

CHAPTER 2

Supply Chain Risk Management Process

The old way of organizing business was by vertical integration with modern cross-organizational supply chains. John D. Rockefeller and Standard Oil, U.S. Steel, Alcoa, and others took the idea of system logistics developed by the military and applied it to their business operations, taking the approach that if there was any profit to be made in their supply chain, they wanted it. This, of course, also led to their taking on associated risk, but the general attitude at that time was that the better they controlled operations, the more they could control the risks involved. This led to vertical supply chains connecting mines, processing, transportation, and various forms of production to different levels of marketing for massive monopolies. Supply chain decisions involved facilities siting. Mines were fixed by the location of minerals, but refining and other processing plants could be located many places. The cost trade-off usually involved minimizing production costs with transportation costs (logistics), either of raw materials to processing plants or output to consumers.

The modern way of conducting business is quite different. The vertically integrated relationships of 19th- and early 20th-century businesses have been replaced by cooperative arrangements of supply chain members. Thus, in addition to facility location, supplier selection becomes important. The focus is on being more competitive, and thus emphasizing services related to the products being made. There also is an emphasis on linking together specialists, with a dynamic integration of often reasonably independent entities working together to deliver goods and services. Goods and services are less distinguishable, making the old dichotomy of operations passé. The commoditization of products and services has evolved to consider not only price, but quality, delivery performance, reliability, and risk.

Global competition, technological change, and the continual search for competitive advantage have motivated risk management in supply chains.[1] This is because integration of multiple organizations in the supply chain has added new types of risks over and above those found in traditional vertically integrated organizations. Supply chains are now often complex systems of networks, reaching hundreds or thousands of participants around the globe (e.g., Walmart or Dell). The term has been used both at the strategic level (coordination and collaboration) and the tactical level (management of logistics across functions and between businesses).[2] In this sense, risk management can focus on identification of better ways and means of accomplishing organizational objectives rather than simply preservation of assets or risk avoidance. Supply chain risk management is interested in the coordination and collaboration of processes and activities across functions within a network of organizations. Supply chains enable manufacturing outsourcing to take advantage of global relative advantages, as well as increase product variety. There are many risks inherent in this more open, dynamic system.

A process is a way to get required work done. Risk is an abstract concept, requiring imagination concerning what can go wrong. Risk management carries that idea a step further—developing ways to deal with contingent risks should they occur. As with any business decision, costs of protection need to be weighed against the benefits provided by risk mitigation.

Risk Management Process in Supply Chains

Risk management in supply chains is important because of the magnitude of disruption. Land supply chains need reliable delivery of inputs. Rover had to lay off more than 1,000 members of their workforce when a key supplier went insolvent and thus ceased production of Rover's inputs. Dole was similarly affected by Hurricane Mitch hitting their banana plantations in Central America in 1998, cutting delivery of fruit. September 11, 2001, suspended air traffic, leading Ford Motor Company to close five plants for several days.[3] Many things can disrupt supply chains. The efficiency gained by connecting to low-cost producers involves risks.

A typical process applied to the supply chain risk management process includes risk identification, risk assessment, risk avoidance, and risk mitigation. These steps provide a framework under which robust strategies can be designed to cope with the many risks involved in global supply chains.

Risk Identification

Risks in supply chains can include operational risks and disruptions. Operational risks involve inherent uncertainties for supply chain elements such as customer demand, supply, and cost. Disruption risks come from disasters (natural in the form of floods, hurricanes, tornadoes, and the like, and man-made in the form of terrorist attacks, wars, and meltdowns at nuclear power plants) and from economic crises (currency reevaluations, strikes, shifting market prices). Most quantitative analyses and methods are focused on operational risks. Disruptions are more dramatic, less predictable, and thus are much more difficult to model. Risk management planning and response for disruption are usually qualitative.

Lean manufacturing gains efficiencies by reducing inventory stocks, which serve as a form of insurance against supply disruption. The media often blames lean systems for disrupted production. However, even when safety stocks were larger, there were still supply disruptions. The added risk due to lean safety stocks is probably more than offset by the gains in reduced inventory expense.

Risk Assessment

Theoretically risk has been viewed as applying to those cases where odds are known (like casinos), while uncertainty applies to those cases where odds are not known (like an investment in a new venture). Risk is a preferable basis for decision making, but life often presents decision makers with cases of uncertainty. The issue is further complicated in that perfectly rational decision makers may have radically different approaches to risk. Research into cognitive psychology has found that managers are often insensitive to probability estimates of possible outcomes and tend to ignore possible events that they consider to be unlikely. Furthermore, managers tend to pay little attention to uncertainty involved with positive outcomes. They tend to focus on critical performance targets, which makes their responses to risk contingent upon context. Some approaches to theoretical decision making prefer objective treatment of risk through quantitative scientific measures following normative ideas of how humans should make decisions. Business involves high levels of uncertainty (e.g., data may not be available) and consideration of multiple (often conflicting) factors, making qualitative approaches based upon perceived managerial risk more appropriate.

Because accurate measures of factors such as probability are often lacking, robust strategies (those that are more likely to enable effective responses under a wide range of circumstances) are often attractive to risk managers. Strategies are efficient if they enable a firm to deal with operational risks efficiently regardless of major disruptions. Strategies are resilient if they enable a firm to keep operating despite major disruptions. Supply chain risk can arise from many sources, including product availability, distance from sources, industry capacity, changes in technology and labor markets, financial instability, and management turnover, as well as those risk categories listed as internal in Table 1.2.

Risk Avoidance

The oldest form of risk avoidance is probably insurance, purchasing some level of financial security from an underwriter. Insurance focuses on the financial aspects of risk and is reactive, providing some recovery after a negative experience. Delta Airlines insurance premiums for terrorism increased from $2 million in 2001 to $152 million in 2002.[4] A major risk is the loss of customers due to supply change disruption.

Supply chain risks can be buffered by a variety of methods. Purchasing is usually assigned the responsibility of controlling costs and ensuring the continuity of supply. Buffers in the form of inventories exist to provide some risk reduction, at a cost of higher inventory holding costs. Traditional practice, relying upon extra inventory, multiple suppliers, expediting, and frequent supplier changes, produces high transaction costs, long purchase fulfillment cycle times, and expensive rush orders. Newer risk management approaches, drawing on practices such as supply chain alliances, e-procurement, just-in-time delivery, increased coordination, and other techniques, provide more visibility in supply chain operations. There may be higher prices incurred for goods, and increased security issues, but supply chain risks are reduced.

Risk Mitigation

There are both strategic and tactical aspects involved in supply chain risk. Strategically a network design of supply chain participants can enable better control of supply risks through activities such as finding alternative supply sources in times of emergency. Strategies such as product pricing and rollovers can control demand to a degree. Greater product variety can strategically protect against product risks. And systems providing greater information visibility across supply chain members can enable better coping with risks. Tactical decisions include supplier selection and order allocation (including contractual arrangements); demand control over time, markets, and products; product promotion; and information sharing, vendor-managed inventory systems, and collaborative planning, forecasting, and replenishment.

Supply Chain Risk Categories

Basic risk mitigation approaches for supply chains focus on the sources of risk: management of uncertainty with respect to supply, demand, product management, and information management.

Supply Management

Cost advantages are available to supply chain core organizations from the outsourcing of noncore functions. There are a number of factors involved in supply chain networks. Besides options concerning network design and relationships, decisions need to be made concerning which sources to select, how to allocate orders, and what contractual relationships are needed.

The design of an effective supply chain network must configure the network (link suppliers, manufacturing facilities, distribution centers, warehouses, etc.), assign products to facilities, assign customers to appropriate facilities, and plan how much and when each facility is to produce and ship.

There are many things that can and have gone wrong with the supply side of supply chains. A fire at a Toyota supplier facility forced Toyota to shut down 18 plants for nearly two weeks in February 1997, at an estimated cost of $195 million along with an estimated cost in lost sales of $325 million. On March 17, 2000, a high-voltage electrical line was struck by lightning, leading to a fire in a Royal Philips Electronics fabrication line in their Albuquerque, New Mexico, radio frequency identification (RFID) chip plant. The fire was extinguished in ten minutes. However, eight trays of silicon wafers were destroyed that would have supported several thousand cell phones. This affected both Ericsson and Nokia, major European cell phone manufacturers. Furthermore, Philips estimated that it would take a week to clean up and return to full production, and notified both Ericsson and Nokia to that effect. Ericsson did not perceive a major problem in one week's disruption of delivery, so took no action. Nokia, on the other hand, felt that it would take Philips longer to recover production. Nokia took action to find alternative suppliers. Nokia also worked with Philips to arrange for alternative supplies from Philips's facilities in the Netherlands and Shanghai. Nokia also redesigned some chips to avoid needing Philips chips. Nokia had to reconfigure their design slightly, but they were able to smoothly satisfy customer demand and actually strengthen their market position.[5] Nokia was able to prosper during this period, with profits rising 42% and global market share rising 30% in the third quarter of 2000.[6] Ericsson, meanwhile, suffered a second quarter operating loss of $200 million in its mobile phone division.

The northeast region of the United States suffered an electrical grid blackout in 2003 that left 50 million people from Ohio, Pennsylvania, and New Jersey north through Ontario, Canada, without power for some 30 minutes. While essential services were maintained by the 20% of the electrical system that was still functioning, passenger rail transport was interrupted, and there was a disruption in international air transport as well as financial markets. The blackout was attributed to trees hitting a power line in Ohio. Other disasters, with much greater disruption to supply chains, include hurricanes, earthquakes, terrorism, and political instability. The cost incurred to U.S. companies from one day's supply chain disruption has been estimated to be in the $50 million to $100 million range.[7]

These examples demonstrate the risk impact on supply chain profitability and demonstrate the need to be prepared with contingency plans and implement them quickly, as Nokia did.

Supplier (vendor) evaluation is a very important operational decision. Decisions must be made when selecting which suppliers to employ, as well as decisions with respect to quantities to order from each supplier. With the increase in outsourcing and the opportunities provided by electronic business to tap worldwide markets, these decisions are becoming ever more complex.

Operational risks in supply chain order allocation include uncertainties in demands, supply yields, lead times, and costs. Thus not only do specific suppliers need to be selected, the quantities purchased from them need to be determined on a recurring basis.

Supply chains provide many valuable benefits to their members, but also create problems of coordination that manifest themselves in the "bullwhip" effect.[8] Information system coordination can reduce some of the negative manifestations of the bullwhip effect, but there still remains the issue of profit sharing. Decisions that are optimal for one supply chain member often have negative impacts on the profitability of the entire supply chain.

Demand Management

Predicting the market response to new offerings is highly challenging. Coca-Cola introduced New Coke in 1985, anticipating an exciting new product revenue stream. However, they encountered a mass revolt on the part of the Coca-Cola buying community. Coca-Cola didn't really suffer, as there was increased demand for their old product, but accurately predicting consumer response is challenging. Older readers may remember that Ford Motor Company encountered a similar problem with their Edsel in 1958, which they expected to be hugely popular. However, car buyers of that time were not positively impressed.

Demand management approaches include using data and models to identify strategies using price to change demand. Other strategies include shifting demand over time, across markets, or across products. Power companies, for instance, often charge different rates at different times of the day. Walmart (at least in the past) charged different prices for products sold in stores located in different locations in the same city. Procter & Gamble offers a portfolio of products at different prices with different implied quality. Demand management is one of the aims of advertising and other promotional activities; however, it has long been known as one of the most difficult things to predict over time.

Product Management

Some of the risks encountered by producers involve changes in demand for various reasons. The food industry has one of the more predictable demands in the world, but even they face changes in the demand for specific items. This demand has recently been dramatically affected by scares concerning food safety, including spinach, cherry tomatoes, and many other grocery products. Mad cow disease still concerns the world, especially in South Korea and Japan.

An effective strategy to manage product risk is variety, which can be used to increase market share to serve distinct segments of a market. The basic idea is to diversify products to meet the specific needs of each market segment. However, while this would be expected to increase revenues and market share, it will lead to increased manufacturing and inventory costs.

Various ways to deal with the potential inefficiencies in product variety include Dell's make-to-order strategy. This strategy doesn't waste time or money assembling a product until an order is received. Dell has a very flexible production system enabling them to make-to-order, a core competence that has been very profitable for them. They also don't waste money on inventory, although they do create inventory problems for their suppliers, who are required to provide materials on-call. Walmart has also been very efficient in this respect in the retail industry.

Information Management

E-business has brought us an entirely new business climate, with the ability to electronically generate retail data. Many service organizations and retail outlets generate masses of data. Grocery stores generate large amounts of data with every purchase. Bar coding has made checkout very convenient for retail establishments. Walmart and other retailers have extended electronic data generation to include RFID, allowing tracking of a product's physical location in real time. The electronic age involves data on a very large scale.

Successful retail organizations in the 21st century consider service to the customer to be their focus. Information technology (IT) systems applied across supply chains enable retail organizations to provide better service. A variety of control schemas have evolved to control supply networks. The traditional uncoordinated supply chains of the 1980s, with no information sharing and independent inventory control policies, led to the infamous "bullwhip" phenomenon. The bullwhip phenomenon occurs because of overestimation of demand induced by the lumpiness of orders from downstream elements of the supply chain. An obvious first step in reducing the inefficiencies caused by the bullwhip effect was to increase information sharing across the supply chain. In a short-season environment, the benefits of improved forecasting and production planning have been suggested as solutions.[9] More complete information sharing and coordination systems have also been proposed.[10]

Supply Chain Coordination Systems

There are a number of systems that have been used to coordinate networks of suppliers and retailers in their delivery of products to consumers. Walmart has been a pioneer in all of these systems of coordination, but many other organizations use them.

Efficient Consumer Response

The first type of coordination among supply chain members to alleviate bullwhip risk is information exchange (efficient consumer response), including action plans to enable forecast alignment for long-term and capacity planning.[11] This planning improves visibility and thus makes demand more predictable. Faster transfer of information across organizations has not avoided all difficulties, however.[12] Problems include slow item-level replenishment as opposed to fast order placement. Retailers in the grocery industry carry tens of thousands (if not hundreds of thousands) of specific stock-keeping units. In this complex environment, an order may be placed after a product is sold. Furthermore, small items are often delivered in bulk packages, which can lead to difficulties. On the supplier side, short lead times and high service-level requirements squeeze out most reaction time. If extremely accurate information at a detailed level is not available, the system almost guarantees stock-out situations. Avoiding such stock-outs through higher inventories in turn eliminates most of the benefits of a well-managed inventory system.

Vendor-Managed Inventory

Vendor-managed inventory (VMI) involves the supplier assuming the responsibility for management of a retailer's inventory. We have all seen this in grocery stores. Companies such as Pepsi, Coke, and popular potato chip producers own the product until it crosses the checkout counter. The grocery store is thus a broker between the producer and the consumer. The value of VMI is that the producer has more control over product placement, and usually signs contracts restricting competition. This is called channel coordination. Based on advanced information through electronic data interchange (EDI) or the Internet, the supplier controls the stock at the retailer. VMI has been analytically shown to yield superior performance over traditional supply chain systems. VMI optimizes the overall profits of the supply chain, as it is superior to traditional local inventory management.[13] VMI can gain efficiencies through shipment consolidation. It also allows retailers to expand the assortment of products they carry in a given retail space, thus improving brand profitability for both retailer and vendor.

VMI has been adopted by many firms. However, VMI has been abandoned in some cases.[14] One possible weakness is insufficient visibility over the entire supply chain. VMI has been found to work well when manufacturers supply large volumes of frequently replenished products under relatively stable sales conditions. Advertising can lead to these conditions. VMI has also been found to perform better when consumers are unlikely to purchase substitutes in cases of stock-outs. But high levels of demand volatility lead to excessive inventories, the same problem that exists in traditional retail inventory control through the bullwhip effect. However, when substitution is attractive, VMI can lead to poorer performance than traditional retailer-managed inventory.[15]

Continuous Replenishment

Continuous replenishment (CR) is an automatic replenishment program, where a retailer's inventory is restocked by the supplier based upon actual product usage and stock level information provided by the retailer. Walmart piloted CR in 1995, and it has been used by larger U.S. and UK retailers. Retailers provide point-of-sale data to suppliers, making it possible to base inventory decisions on sales forecasts rather than inventory level variations. CR enhanced VMI by requiring supply chain members to share more information and data, and to utilize common systems and use common performance measures. This promoted joint decision making, accountability, and incentives for performance. CR has been cited in improving customer service levels and inventory turnover.[16] However, because CR does not necessarily cover inventories throughout the supply chain, it still can include gaps. Manufacturers' predictions of future retail events is the major missing feature of CR. Excess inventory seems to be shifted from retailers and distributors to manufacturers. While CR improved VMI, further benefits were available.

Collaborative Planning, Forecasting, and Replenishment

Collaborative planning, forecasting, and replenishment (CPFR) was the next step after CR and has been applied in the drug, grocery, apparel, and other industries.[17] The manufacturer and retailer exchange marketplace information to develop customer-specific plans to substantially reduce inventory. Promotion schedules, point-of-sale data, and inventory data are shared to enable the shortening of lead times and the integration of forecasting and replenishment. Thus total visibility is obtained and changing demand patterns can be considered.

The way in which information is exchanged yields a number of benefits. For retailers, these include increased sales, faster response times to orders, and higher service levels despite lower inventories, which in turn lead to lower costs from obsolescence and deterioration. Manufacturers benefit through increased sales, higher fill rates for orders, faster cycle times, lower capacity requirements, and lower product inventories. There are fewer stocking points needed over the supply chain, improved forecast accuracy, and, overall, lower expenses throughout the system.

Boeing and Alcoa provide an example of the implementation of CPFR.[18] The problem in this case, involving Alcoa-supplied aluminum products for Boeing airplanes, included rail transportation that involved unreliable delivery dates. The presence of minimum quantities in multiple bundles distorted forecasts. The two companies planned several supply chain elements to overcome these difficulties. Information systems were integrated, allowing real-time information exchange. Operations were tightly linked between supplier and manufacturer. Lean manufacturing principles were applied. Close cooperation led to an atmosphere with high levels of trust. Boeing sent weekly electronic forecasts and inventory counts to Alcoa and used its enterprise resource planning (ERP) system to generate electronic purchase orders for raw materials. Alcoa implemented a vendor-managed inventory system and improved forecast visibility in their system. Alcoa also had to change its order entry process to accept Boeing orders. The electronic forecasting system was credited with expediting information exchange. Boeing carefully checked its forecasting and identified modifications to data obtained from their ERP system that were needed to provide Alcoa with more accurate data. The greater degree of forecasting accuracy enabled Alcoa to make more efficient production decisions. A blanket purchase order for one year was used to override the ERP-generated purchasing system. Forecasts were aggregated by week.

CPFR has encountered some barriers. As with VMI, systems need to be compatible across organizations, and the more organizations involved, the more restrictive this requirement is.

Examples of Supply Chain Resilience

Natural disasters by definition are surprises causing a great deal of damage and inconvenience. Some things we do to ourselves, such as revolutions, terrorist attacks, and wars. Terrorism led to the gassing of the Japanese subway system, 9/11/2001 attack, and bombings of Spanish and British transportation systems. Nature does many things to us—volcanic eruptions, tsunamis, hurricanes, and tornados. The 2003 SARS virus disrupted public and business activities, particularly in Asia. The H1N1 virus has sharpened the awareness of the response system worldwide. Some disasters combine human and natural causes. We have developed low-pollution, low-cost electricity through nuclear energy, such as at Three-Mile Island in Pennsylvania and Chernobyl. We have built massive chemical plants to produce low cost chemicals, such as at Bhopal, India.

While natural disasters come as surprises, we can still be prepared. In some cases, such as Hurricane Katrina, we have premonitions to warn us, but we never completely know the extent of what is going to happen. Lee and Preston[19] provided a very good review of high-impact, low-probability events, focusing on the analysis of the Eyjafjallajökull volcano. Other examples include Hurricane Katrina in New Orleans, as well as the Japanese earthquake and tsunami of 2011. What we don't do to ourselves in the form of wars and economic catastrophes, nature trumps with overwhelming natural disasters.

The World Economic Forum published an analysis of supply chain resilience in January 2013.[20] Supply chains are threatened externally (natural disasters and demand shocks), within systems (oil dependence, information disruptions), and by general systemic risks (cyber risk, insurance risk). Table 2.1 shows supply chain disruptions in 2012.

Table 2.1. Supply Chain Disruptions in 2012

Date	Event	Impact
Early 2012	Thai floods	Automotive and high-tech industries
Mid-year	U.S. drought	Crop failure, low water on Mississippi
	Horn of Africa —famine	Difficulty in logistics through militia-controlled areas
November 2012	Hurricane Sandy	Closed ports and airports in Northeast U.S.— worst fuel shortages since the 1970s

Other disruptions have long-term effects, such as, 1973 saw an Arab oil embargo that still disrupts the world economy. This petroleum-industry factor was enhanced by the 1980 Iranian Revolution. Financial crises in Asia in the late 1990s, a dot-com bubble in 2001, and a global financial crisis in 2008 still grip world economic activity in 2014, joining the petroleum factor. Supply chains in short have had to withstand tremendous shocks, from nature as well as from artifacts.

Robust Strategies

Robust supply chain strategies that have proven useful in coping with supply chain disruption include the following:[21]

1. **Postponement** relies on design concepts, including standardization, commonality, and modular design, to delay the point of product differentiation. A more generic product is produced based on aggregate demand, applying customization to specific products later in the production cycle. This enables a more flexible response to specific product demands. Nokia's response to the Philips fire in 2000 was an example of this strategy, which has also been used by Xilinx (producer of programmable logic chips), Hewlett-Packard (who utilized postponement by mass-producing a generic workstation using production to stock), and Benetton (who produced undyed sweaters that were later dyed as needed to fill customer orders). Postponement improves a company's ability to manage supplies and provides greater product flexibility.

2. **Strategic stock** is used to gain the benefits of safety stock for key items without the expense incurred in excessive inventories for all items. Examples include Toyota, who inventoried cars at key distribution locations to ensure an ample supply in particular regions, and Sears, who did the same thing with appliances. This allows higher customer service levels without excessive inventory holding costs. Similar strategies are used by the Centers for Disease Control for medical supplies. Strategic stocks increase product availability, enabling quicker response.

3. The **flexible supply base** strategy mitigates risks from sole sourcing through multiple suppliers. Hewlett-Packard used plants in Washington State and in Singapore for inkjet printers, relying upon the less expensive Singapore plant for base volume, and the Washington plant to satisfy demand fluctuations. This enabled some volume slack to cope with supply disruptions through increasing supply flexibility.

4. The **make-and-buy** strategy is the same idea as the flexible supply base strategy, only it includes external production as an alternative source. Hewlett-Packard used this strategy for DeskJet printers, which were primarily outsourced to a Malaysian manufacturer, with

the Singapore factory handling a portion of the production. Zara is famous for applying this principle in fashion clothing. The benefits are the same as with a flexible supply base.

5. **Economic supply incentives** can be used even if production cannot be shifted. The U.S. market supply for flu vaccine of a specific type was reduced because of uncertain demand and government price pressure. That left two vaccine producers in the United States. In October 2005 one of these producers was suspended because of bacterial contamination in their production line, leading to an expected shortage of 48 million flu shots, and subsequent rationing to high-risk groups. The use of economic supply incentives could increase participation in this market, averting future shortages. In a similar example, Intercon Japan had one key supplier and became concerned about the supplier's monopoly position. Intercon Japan offered economic incentives to Nagoya Steel to develop a new steel process to produce their cable connectors, including minimum order quantities, technical advice, and market demand information. This enabled Intercon Japan to keep price pressure on its original supplier, achieving increased product availability and enabling them to quickly adjust order quantities.

6. **Flexible transportation** is a strategy that provides assurance of delivery. It can be accomplished in a variety of ways, including multimodal transportation. Seven-Eleven Japan encouraged its logistics partner to diversify into a system of trucks, motorcycles, bicycles, ships, and helicopters. This enabled Seven-Eleven Japan to rush delivery of rice balls to Kobe earthquake victims in 1995. Multicarrier transportation ensures a continuous flow of materials. Alliances of cargo airlines have been able to quickly switch carriers when faced with regional political disruptions and also allow lower-cost delivery. The use of multiple routes is a third transportation strategy, enabling bypassing of temporary bottlenecks. When U.S. West Coast ports were shut down in 2002, shipments from Asia used the Panama Canal to reach East Coast ports.

7. **Dynamic pricing and promotion** are forms of revenue management strategies. Airline yield management systems are a manifestation of this strategy, providing gains of almost $1 billion for American Airlines.[22] Dell also applied low-cost upgrade options to customers

when faced with supply disruptions after the Taiwanese earthquake in 1999 (mentioned earlier). Revenue management increases control over product demand, enabling the firm to influence customer product selection.

8. **Dynamic assortment planning** is a strategy based on influencing consumer product demand by display location. Supermarkets manipulate demand on a routine basis through product positioning, allowing them to increase control of product demand.

9. **Silent product rollover** involves slow leaking of new products without formal announcements. This encourages customers to select available products instead of asking for products that have been phased out or are out of stock. Examples of this strategy are Swatch, which produces each product once, and Zara, which launches new fashion collections without fanfare. Thus all products are substitutes, which expedites dealing with demand fluctuations as well as coping with supply or demand disruption.

Any strategy will have downsides. The costs and benefits in each specific case are often difficult to quantify, especially due to the factor of competitiveness. Each organization needs to consider its overall business strategy. Firms that desire to focus on a limited number of products for strategic reasons will find little value in the postponement strategy. Walmart strategically emphasizes a low-cost strategy, and thus dynamic pricing and promotion make little sense for their situation. Strategies also need to be feasible. During the 2002 longshoreman's strike on the U.S. West Coast, a Toyota–General Motors venture relied on a six-day inventory to deal with disruptions. However, the strike lasted longer than that, making it impossible to unload components sitting in West Coast ports for rerouting.

Conclusion

Supply chains have become important elements in the conduct of global business, and we all gain from allowing broader participation of those with relative advantages. Alliances can serve as safety nets by providing alternative sources, routes, or products for their members. Risk exposure within supply chains can be reduced by reducing lead times, which can be accomplished by collocation of suppliers at production facilities.

Supply chain organizations have a number of responses available to manage and mitigate risk. Insurance is risk mitigation, by definition. With respect to outsourcing, different levels of coordination can still be applied, although the term outsourcing implies a looser degree of control. Still, organizations such as Walmart require their supply chain participants to have compatible information systems.[24] Walmart has also worked toward greater use of technology, such as RFID. Other responses include the development of closer relationships with outsourcing agencies, imposition of performance standards, joint training, joint strategy development, and marketing.[25] Recent trends include more independent responses, such as insurance and contractual standards, and more cooperative efforts (such as shared information or the development of closer relationships).[26]

This chapter has discussed some of the many risks associated with supply chains. A rational process of dealing with these risks includes assessment of what can go wrong, quantitative measurement of risk likelihood and severity, qualitative planning to cover a broad set of possible risks, and contingency planning. A wide variety of available supply chain risk-reduction strategies were reviewed, with cases of real applications.

While no supply chain network can expect to anticipate all future disruptions, it can put in place a process to reduce exposure and impact. This planning will provide a better organizational response, in keeping with organizational objectives.

CHAPTER 3

Risk Matrices in Supply Chain Risk Management

In chapter 2 I discussed the role of risk identification in the risk management process. In this chapter I will expand this discussion to include looking at risk matrices as tools to aid in identifying risk.

It is useful for organizations to begin by assessing their **risk appetite**. No organization can avoid risk. Nor should they insure against every risk. Organizations exist to take on risks in areas where they have developed the capability to cope with that risk. However, they cannot cope with every risk, so top management needs to identify the risks they expect to face and those risks they are willing to assume (and profit from successfully coping).

The **risk identification** process needs to consider risks of all kinds. Examples of typical risks faced by organizations including supply chains are outlined in Table 3.1.

Each manager should be responsible for ongoing risk identification and control within their area of responsibility. Once risks are identified, a risk matrix can be developed. Risk matrices will be explained in the next section. The risk management process is the control aspect of those risks that are identified. The adequacy of this process depends on assigning appropriate responsibilities by role. It can be monitored by a risk-screening committee at a high level within the organization that monitors significant new markets and products. The **risk review** process includes a systematic internal audit, often outsourced to third-party providers responsible for ensuring that the enterprise risk management structure functions as designed.

Table 3.1. Enterprise Risk Management Framework

Strategic risks	• A process to identify potential changes in markets, economic conditions, regulations, and demographic changes and their impacts on the business • Consider both the short-run and long-run impact in new product design • Consider the service aspect of the product line • Adequate research and development (R&D) investment to keep up with competitors' product development • Controls sufficient to satisfy regulatory audits
Operations risks	• Train and encourage the use of rational decision-making models • Develop a master list of vendor relationships, with assurance each provides value • Adequate segregation of duties • Adequate cash and marketable securities controls • Documented and tested financial models • Documented strategic plan for technology expenditures
Legal risks	• Audit patent requirements to avoid competitor abuse as well as litigation • Inventory of legal agreements and audit of compliance • Protect customer privacy in legal agreements • Identify disturbing litigation patterns • Ensure product quality sufficient to avoid class action suits and loss of reputation
Credit risks	• Maintain key statistics to monitor credit trends • Manage settlement risks • Provide sufficient collateral • Provide an incentive compensation program that adequately rewards profitability rather than volume • Monitor exposure to foreign entities
Market risks	• Develop a documented funding plan • Analyze asset/liability management model assumptions • Provide a contingency funding plan for extreme events • Analyze core deposits for price and cash flow

Risk Matrix

A risk matrix provides a two-dimensional (or higher) picture of risk for firm departments, products, projects, or other items of interest. It is intended to provide a means to better estimate the probability of success or failure and identify those activities that require greater control. One example might be for a manufacturer's product line, as shown in Table 3.2.

Table 3.2. Product Risk Matrix

	Likelihood of risk low	Likelihood of risk medium	Likelihood of risk high
Level of risk high	Hedge	Avoid	Avoid
Level of risk medium	Internal controls	Hedge	Hedge
Level of risk low	Accept	Internal controls	Internal controls

Risk matrices have been applied in many contexts. One example, in the medical field, is a risk matrix for child development focused on predicting basic cognitive, motor, and noncognitive abilities based on the two dimensions of organic risk factors and psychosocial risk factors.[1] Risk matrices have also been used by the National Health Service Litigation Authority for clinical risk management in the United Kingdom.[2] Traffic light colors are often used to categorize risks into three (or more) categories, quickly identifying combinations of frequency and consequence calling for the greatest attention. Table 3.3 shows a possible risk matrix of medical events.

Table 3.3. Risk Matrix of Medical Events

	Consequence insignificant	Consequence minor	Consequence moderate	Consequence major	Consequence catastrophic
Likelihood almost certain	Green	Amber	Red	Red	Red
Likelihood likely	Green	Amber	Amber	Red	Red
Likelihood possible	Green	Amber	Amber	Amber	Red
Likelihood unlikely	Green	Green	Amber	Amber	Red
Likelihood rare	Green	Green	Green	Amber	Amber

In Table 3.3, green indicates no special action is required. The organization should identify contingent alternatives, but not drop current plans or choices. Amber indicates a greater risk, calling for alternative sources of supply or alternative transportation routes. Additional insurance (in either the literal or analogous sense) should be considered, although cost–benefit analysis is called for. Red indicates a need to take action to avoid the expected risk. This could mean switching to new sources, dropping a product line, recalling a product, or obtaining a new transportation alternative. Red calls for spending money to minimize loss.

Caveats

While risk matrices have proven useful, they can be misused, as can any tool.[3] Table 3.4 shows an example risk matrix from the Federal Highway Administration. In Table 3.4, green indicates that projects should be postponed and funds allocated to more critical projects. Yellow indicates projects for replacement of existing facilities are needed, but are not critical. Red indicates that projects are needed to replace existing facilities as soon as possible.

Table 3.4. Risk Matrix for Federal Highway Administration (2006)

	Very low impact	Low impact	Medium impact	High impact	Very high impact
Very high probability	Green	Yellow	Red	Red	Red
High probability	Green	Yellow	Red	Red	Red
Medium probability	Green	Green	Yellow	Red	Red
Low probability	Green	Green	Yellow	Red	Red
Very low probability	Green	Green	Green	Yellow	Red

Source: Cox (2008).

Some characteristics should be present in all risk matrices:

1. No red cell should share an edge with a green cell.
2. No red cell can occur in the left column or in the bottom row.
3. There must be at least three colors.
4. Too many colors give spurious results.

Cox (2008) argues that risk ratings do not necessarily support good resource allocation decisions. This is due to the inherently subjective categorization of uncertain consequences. Thus Cox argues that his theoretical results demonstrate that quantitative and semiquantitative risk matrices (using numbers instead of categories) cannot correctly reproduce risk ratings, especially if frequency and severity are negatively correlated.

The risk matrix is meant to be a tool used to reveal the distribution of risk across a firm's portfolio of products, projects, or activities, and to assign responsibilities or mitigation activities. In Table 3.2, **hedging** activities might include paying for insurance, or in the case of investments, using short-sale activities. **Internal controls** would call for extra managerial effort to quickly identify adverse events and take action (at some cost) to provide greater assurance of acceptable outcomes. Risk matrices can represent continuous scales.

Supply Chain Risk Management Example

The TECHNEAU project applied risk assessment to six European and African drinking water systems in 2007–2008, seeking the application and evaluation of the applicability of hazard identification and risk assessment. One of these studies was about the water supply of the Upper Mnyameni in the Eastern Cape region of South Africa.[4]
The process used included:

- **Risk Analysis**—definition of scope, identification of hazards, and both qualitative and quantitative estimation of risks
- **Risk Evaluation**—definition of tolerable levels for water quality and water quantity
- **Risk Reduction/Control**—decisions leading to risk treatment and monitoring

These case studies had four objectives:

1. Identification of drinking water system risks
2. Investigation of risks of failure for water supplies as well as risks of insufficient supply
3. Evaluation of risks and consequences for humans as well as societal development
4. Evaluation of risk assessment methods

Risk matrices were used to rank likelihood and consequences based on inputs from experts of Amatola Water, local water supply administrators.

Water System

There are many water resources in South Africa, with widely varying quality by locality. Coastal and eastern regions receive ample rainfall, but inland and western locales suffer from low levels of precipitation. Therefore, rainfall is usually collected in dams. Water treatment facilities are provided by many small treatment plants, which are more expensive than a centralized facility. The region served in the rural area in the Amatola Mountains in the Eastern Cape province has low income and very high unemployment, reaching 80 percent.

Health Effects Risk Matrix

The study involved generation of risk scenarios. The 11 scenarios identified by brainstorming were:

1. High turbidity causing ineffective chlorination
2. Contaminated taps due to animals
3. Inadequate hygiene due to low water availability in homes
4. Contaminated groundwater leaking into pipes
5. Poor water storage
6. Lack of treated water leading to use of untreated water
7. High turbidity when water treatment facilities were unmanned, resulting in high bacteria
8. Ineffective mixing of chlorine resulting in high bacteria

9. Sabotage of a part of the system

10. Incorrect action due to lack of operator skill

11. Pump failure due to unmanned plant

Each of these scenarios was ranked on a 1–5 scale by Amatola Water experts. Consequences are shown on the column headings in Table 3.5, and the scenario ranking results placed in the appropriate box.

Table 3.5. Risk Matrix for Health Consequences

	Little or no health risk	Minor health risk	Considerable health risk	Potential for major health risk	Major health risk (illness and death)
Frequent			2,5		
Occasional		6			
Possible					
Rare				3	
Has not occurred	1,4,9	7,8,10	11		

Table 3.5 shows major risks from scenarios 2 (contaminated taps from animal activity) and 5 (poor water storage). Intermediate risk scenarios were 3 (inadequate hygiene due to low water availability in homes) and 6 (water shortage resulting in the use of untreated water). The other seven scenarios fell into the region of low risk, all because the experts had not experienced these possible events.

Table 3.6 gives a second risk matrix showing scenarios in terms of the number of people affected.

Table 3.6. Risk Matrix for People Affected

	1-9 people	10-29 people	30-249 people	250-1250 people	Over 1250 people
Frequent	5	2			
Occasional					6
Possible					
Rare					3
Has not occurred				11	1,4,7,8,9,10

Table 3.6 shows that of the two serious risks identified in Table 3.5, one (scenario 5, poor water storage) applies to a minimal number of individuals, while scenario 2 (contaminated taps from animal activity) affects an expected 10–29 people. The minor health risk of scenario 6 (water shortage resulting in use of untreated water) applies to a large number of people, as does scenario 3 (inadequate hygiene due to low water availability. A final stage of analysis weighted health effects three times as important as the number of people affected. A formulation of total consequence was obtained and used as a basis for ranking water source risk. This ranked the scenarios in the order shown in Table 3.7.

Table 3.7. Calculation of Scenario Risk Ranking

Scenario	Health x 3	People x 1	Weighted	Rank
3—low water usage in homes resulting in poor hygiene	4	5	4.25	1
11—pump failure from lack of personnel	3	4	3.25	2
2—contamination from animal activity	3	2	2.75	3
6—use of untreated water due to shortage	2	5	2.75	3
7—turbidity from lack of personnel	2	5	2.75	3
8—high bacteria from poor chlorine mixing	2	5	2.75	3
10—nonpotable water due to poor training	2	5	2.75	3
5—poor water storage	3	1	2.50	8
1—heavy rainfall leading to high turbidity and bacterial count	1	5	2.00	9
4—contaminated leakage into pipes	1	5	2.00	9
9—sabotage	1	5	2.00	9

These rankings were used to reflect consequence in the final risk matrix, given in Table 3.8.

There was additional activity in the overall risk analysis, but a primary use of the risk matrices was to identify scenarios that needed improvement. Here, scenarios 2, 3, 5, and 6 all were found in the high or intermediate

Table 3.8. Risk Matrix for Consequence and Frequency

	Little or no consequence (Rank 1)	Minor consequence (Rank 1.5–2.4)	Considerable consequence (Rank 2.5–3.5)	Major consequence (Rank 3.5–4.5)	Catastrophic consequence (Rank 5)
Frequent			2,5		
Occasional			6		
Possible					
Rare				3	
Has not occurred		1,4,9	7,8,10,11		

risk areas. The two red rated risks were considered in the unacceptable range, to be reduced as soon as possible. Scenario 2 involved contamination from animal activity, which could be solved by making all water connections inside housing. This was expected to lead to increased demand, so an alternative solution considered was to protect taps from animal contact in their current location. Scenario 5 was poor water storage (use of open buckets or dirty bottles). This risk could be reduced by making all water connections inside housing, as well as by providing information on hygienic water handling. Scenario 3 was inadequate hygiene due to poor water access inside homes. Again, this would be solved by having taps inside housing. Scenario 6 involved the use of untreated water during periods of shortage due to power failure or other causes. Upgrading the power supply was seen as the best solution. The provision of a back-up generator at the water treatment plant was offered as an intermediate solution.

Example Application of a Risk Management Matrix

Yang, Y.-C. (2010). Impact of the container security initiative on Taiwan's shipping industry. Maritime Policy & Management, 37(7), 699–722.

Since September 11, 2001, there has been a tremendous increase in security concerns. This includes transportation routes of supply chains, because of the threats of terrorism through sabotage of shipping. Thus the United States as well as all of the countries that participate in supply chains leading to the United States are extremely concerned with protecting shipping. Half of U.S. imports arrive via shipping, with about nine million containers arriving each year. Such shipping can be used to transport illegal immigrants, smuggled goods, and weapons, but the primary concern is weapons of mass destruction. The Brookings Institute estimated that the expected loss from a detonated weapon of mass destruction could be $1 trillion, and the threat of terrorism has led to a decrease in investment in the United States of 0.2% of gross domestic product.[5] The Yang case reported efforts in Taiwan to identify risks using a risk management matrix considering the severity and frequency of risks, and applying the matrix to select appropriate risk management responses.

In this case, the risk matrix was developed by assessing when to apply one of three risk treatments: For low risk levels, risk would be self-contained, which is a way of saying the firm would self-insure or take on the risk itself. The intermediate response level was to consider insurance and loss reduction actions. For high risk levels, the policy response was to take actions to avoid risk and transfer it to others through contracts or other means.

The two risk matrix dimensions were frequency and severity. Ranges for each were established with the scales shown in Table 3.9. The basis for these scales was interviews with a customs broker, a freight forwarder, and third-party logistics personnel.

Table 3.9. Scales for Container Security Initiative Risk Matrix

Scale	Frequency	Verbal rating	Severity	Verbal rating
1	Once in more-than 3 years	Unlikely	10,000 NTD (New Taiwan Dollars) or less	Slightest
2	Once in 1–3 years	Seldom	10–50,000 NTD	Slight
3	Once in a year	Passable	50–100,000 NTD	Passable
4	Once in 6–12 months	Occasional	100–500,000 NTD	Critical
5	Once in less than 6 months	Regular	Over 500,000 NTD	More critical

Categorization of specific risks was accomplished through questionnaires sent to 40 customs brokers, 30 freight forwarders, and 15 shipping companies in Taiwan. The risk matrix is shown in Table 3.10.

Table 3.10. Taiwanese Shipping Risk Matrix

	Severity 1	Severity 2	Severity 3	Severity 4	Severity 5
Frequency 1	Green	Green	Green	Amber	Amber
Frequency 2	Green	Green	Amber	Amber	Amber
Frequency 3	Green	Green	Amber	Amber	Red
Frequency 4	Green	Amber	Amber	Red	Red
Frequency 5	Amber	Amber	Red	Red	Red

Green implies standard loss prevention practices, implying normal prudent efforts to avoid risks. Amber calls for extra loss prevention effort at some cost, including insurance. Red calls for more drastic action, including actions to avoid risk or transfer it to others. Based on the U.S. container security initiative requiring preinspection of high-risk cargo by X-ray machines, and a rule requiring manifests be sent to U.S. customs authorities 24 hours prior to the ship leaving the source country, 15 risk assessment factors were graded on both frequency and severity scales based on published regulations or on personal interviews with authorities. Table 3.11 shows the results of applying the risk matrix to 15 situations.

Table 3.11. Risk Management Alternative Outcomes

Risk factor	Severity	Frequency	Risk level	Treatment
Shippers must bear responsibility for container inspection and haulage	2.08	3.38	Green	Loss prevention
Cargo can't be shipped on time, Container Security Initiative (CSI) shuts down shipment, injury to shipper reputation	3.26	3.48	Amber	Insurance and loss reduction
Cargo handling time extended 1–3 days by security inspection	2.15	3.28	Green	Loss prevention
Carriers have to charge shippers extra for security handling costs	2.03	3.34	Green	Loss prevention
Cargo may be subject to double inspection, increasing costs	2.31	3.42	Green	Loss prevention

Risk factor	Severity	Frequency	Risk level	Treatment
Cargo late, shut out by customs authority for lack of compliance	3.57	3.55	Red	Avoidance and risk transfer
CSI inspection scope expanded to import containers, extra inspection and shipping expense	2.55	3.40	Amber	Insurance and loss reduction
Shippers have to bear data transmission expense to U.S. Customs	2.20	3.22	Green	Loss prevention
Cargo data transmission requires more lead time	2.23	3.51	Amber	Insurance and loss reduction
Requirement to deliver cargo prior to 48 hours of departure imposes volume storage problems	2.69	3.52	Amber	Insurance and loss reduction
Shipper receives cargo early, decreasing flexibility	2.48	3.68	Amber	Insurance and loss reduction
Lack of uniformity among security regulations increases costs	2.68	3.77	Amber	Insurance and loss reduction
Shipping company requests for export manifest increases cargo owner costs	2.28	3.03	Green	Loss prevention
Other countries adopt 24-hour rule	2.60	3.31	Amber	Insurance and loss reduction
Confidential documents disclosed	2.75	3.43	Amber	Insurance and loss reduction

Severity and frequency scores were the mean scores obtained through the survey sent to professionals. These means were rounded to determine where they fell on the scale in Table 3.10. Survey subjects were given choices ranging from 1 to 5. This case demonstrates how a risk matrix can be developed and applied in the environment of international shipping, which involves ever-increasing risks. The approach can be applied to many risk environments, providing a quick visual method upon which risk treatments can be established.

Conclusion

This chapter presents scoring systems and risk matrices with the idea that they can provide useful tools for planning supply chain operations. The examples given are necessarily brief, but hopefully demonstrate the potential to support a variety of supply chain operations.

Risk matrices have been proposed for many applications, including product innovation,[6] transportation,[7] and shipping security.[8] While the caveats just pointed out need to be kept in mind, risk matrices provide an easy-to-understand, systematic way to initially assess expected risks that can be applied to supply chain risk management.

The idea of color-coded risk matrices is valuable because they provide an easy-to-interpret visual system to communicate threats to the supply chain. There are quantitative methods that have been proposed, but their value depends upon the accuracy of inputs and resulting probabilities.

CHAPTER 4

Supply Chain Selection Decisions

There are many decisions required in supply chain management to balance risk and return. Supply chain management decisions include which sources to work with, which products to offer to customers, and which transportation modes to adopt in specific circumstances. Decisions are also needed for selecting the type of information technology to acquire, whether hiring a consultant is appropriate, the specific vendor from whom software is purchased, and the specific form of software to adopt. I will first cover some basics in structuring hierarchies of criteria and then describe the simple multiattribute rating technique for multicriteria selection decisions. I will then demonstrate with two example decisions: selecting sources to include in a supply chain and selecting from among product design alternatives.

Hierarchy Structuring

Structuring translates an initially ill-defined problem into a set of well-defined elements, relations, and operations. There are a number of good sources explaining the process in detail.[1]

The simplest hierarchy involves *value* as an objective, with available alternatives branching from this *value* node. Hierarchies generally involve additional layers of objectives when the number of branches from any one node exceeds some certain value (see Figure 4.1). Cognitive psychology has found that people are poor at assimilating too many branches.

Next is identification of the overall fundamental objective. The overall objective can be the combination of specific fundamental objectives, such as minimizing costs, minimizing detrimental health impacts, and minimizing negative environmental impacts. Subordinate to fundamental objectives are means objectives—ways to accomplish the fundamental objectives. Means objectives should be mutually exclusive and collectively exhaustive with respect to fundamental objectives. Available alternatives are the bottom level of the hierarchy, measured on all objectives immediately superior. If alternative performance on an objective is not measurable, Keeney (1992) suggests dropping that objective. Value judgments are required for fundamental objectives, and judgments about facts are required for means–ends objectives.

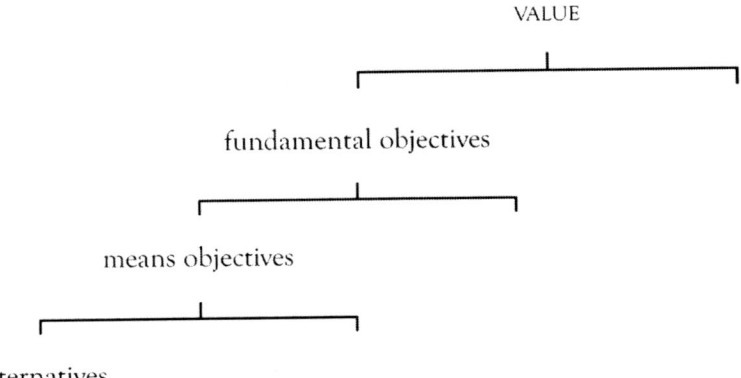

Figure 4.1. Value Hierarchy

Decision makers should not settle for those alternatives that are thrust upon them. The conventional solution process is to generate alternative solutions to a problem and then focus on objectives. This framework tends to suppose an environment where decision makers are powerless to do anything but choose among given alternatives. It is suggested that a more fruitful approach would be for decision makers to use objectives to create alternatives, based on what the decision makers would like to achieve and why objectives are important.

Neiger, Rotaru, and Churilov (2009) applied Keeney's (1992) value-focused approach to supply chain risk identification.[2] I hypothesize a supply chain participant producing products for a multinational retailer. We can start looking for overall values in Table 4.1. The first focus is on the purpose of the business—the product. Product characteristics of importance include its quality, meeting specifications, cost, and delivery. In today's business environment, we argue that service is part of the product. We represent that in our hierarchy with the concept of manufacturability and deliverability to consumers (which reflects the life cycle value to the customer). The operation of the supply chain is considered next, under the phrase "management," which reflects the ability of the supply chain to communicate and to be agile in response to changes. There are also external risks, which we cluster into the three areas of political (regulation, as well as war and terrorism), economic (overall economic climate, as well as the behavior of the specific market being served), and natural disaster. Each of these hierarchical elements can then be used to identify specific risks for a given supply chain situation.

The next step in multiattribute analysis is to generate the alternatives. There are a number of decisions that might be made, including vendor selection, plant siting, information system selection, or the decision to enter specific markets by region or country. For some of these, there may be binary decisions (enter a country's market or not) or there may be a number of variants (including different degrees of entering a specific market). In vendor selection and plant siting, there may be very many alternatives. Usually multiattribute analysis focuses on two to seven alternatives that are selected as most appropriate through some screening process. Part of the benefit of value analysis is that better alternatives can be designed as part of the hierarchical development, seeking better solutions that perform well on all features.

The simple multiattribute rating theory (SMART)[3] can be used with spreadsheet support and is usually the easiest method to use. I will demonstrate using SMART for a decision involving site selection of a plant within a supply chain.

Table 4.1. Value Hierarchy for Supply Chain Risk

Top level	Second level	Third level
Product	Quality	
	Cost	Price
		Investment required
		Holding cost/service level trade-off
	On-time delivery	
Service	Manufacturability	Outsourcing opportunity cost/risk trade-off
		Ability to expand production
		New technology breakthroughs
		Product obsolescence
	Deliverability	Transportation system
		Insurance cost
Management	Communication	Information system breakdown
		Distorted information leading to bullwhip effect
		Forecast accuracy
		Integration
		Viruses/bugs/hackers
	Flexibility	Agility of sources
		Ability to replace sources as needed
	Safety	Plant disaster
	Labor	Risk of strikes, disputes
Political	Government	Customs and regulations
	War and terrorism	
Economic	Overall economy	Economic downturn
		Exchange rate risk
	Specific regional economy	Labor cost influence
		Changes in competitive advantage
	Specific market	Price fluctuation
		Customer demand volatility
		Customer payment
Natural disaster		Uncontrollable disaster
		Diseases, epidemics

The SMART Technique

Edwards (1977) proposed a 10-step technique. These steps include the process of identifying objectives and organizing these objectives into a hierarchy. Guidelines concerning the pruning of these objectives to a reasonable number were provided.

Step 1: Identify the person or organization whose utilities are to be maximized. Edwards argued that the Multiple Attribute Utility Theory (MAUT) can be applied to public decisions in the same manner as was proposed for individual decision making.

Step 2: Identify the issue or issues. Utility depends on the context and purpose of the decision.

Step 3: Identify the alternatives to be evaluated. This step identifies the outcomes of possible actions, a data-gathering process.

Step 4: Identify the relevant dimensions of value for evaluation of the alternatives. It is important to limit the dimensions of value to those that are important for this particular decision. This can be accomplished by restating and combining goals or by omitting less important goals. Edwards argued that it was not necessary to have a complete list of goals. If the weight for a particular goal is quite low, that goal need not be included. There is no precise range of goals for all decisions. However, a range of 8 goals is considered sufficiently large for most cases, and 15 is too many.

Step 5: Rank the dimensions in order of importance. Ranking is a decision task that is easier than developing weights. For decisions made by one person, this step is fairly straightforward. This task is usually more difficult in group environments. However, groups including diverse opinions can provide a more thorough analysis of relative importance, as all sides of the issue are more likely to be voiced. An initial discussion can provide all group members with a common information base. This can be followed by identification of individual judgments of relative ranking.

Step 6: Rate dimensions in order of importance, preserving ratios. The least important dimension is assigned an importance of 10. The next least important dimension is assigned a number reflecting the ratio of relative importance to the least important dimension.

This process is continued, checking implied ratios as each new judgment is made. Since this requires a growing number of comparisons, there is a very practical need to limit the number of dimensions (objectives).

Step 7: Sum the importance weights and divide each by the sum. This step allows normalization of the relative importance of each dimension into weights summing to 1.0.

Step 8: Measure the location of each alternative being evaluated on each dimension. Dimensions are classified into the groups: subjective, partly subjective, and purely objective. For subjective dimensions, an expert in this field would estimate the value of an alternative on a 0–100 scale, with 0 as the minimum plausible value and 100 the maximum plausible value.

Step 9: Calculate utilities for alternatives. $U_j = \Sigma_k w_k u_{jk}$, where U_j is the utility value for alternative j, w_k is the normalized weight for objective k, and u_{jk} is the scaled value for alternative j on dimension k. $\Sigma_k w_k = 1$. The w_k values were obtained from Step 7 and the u_{jk} values were generated in Step 8.

Step 10: Decide. If a single alternative is to be selected, select the alternative with the maximum U_j. If a budget constraint exists, rank order alternatives in the order of U_j / C_j, where C_j is the cost of alternative j. Then alternatives are selected in order of the highest ratio first until the budget is exhausted.

Source Selection

The first supply chain decision we consider involves source, or vendor, selection. Global business opens up the world as potential sources of business. Outsourcing increases some external uncertainties for core supply chain entities (e.g., reliability of supply, compliance with quality) and reduces others (e.g., outsourcing would be expected to yield lower costs, which reduces the probability of losing customers). Table 4.2 is based on supply chain risks related to supply chain outsourcing.

Table 4.2. Supply Chain Risks Assessed for Outsourcing Impact

Supply chain risk	Elaboration	Outsourcing impact
Accounting risk	Risk of ruin	High
Asset impairment risk	Utilization of assets	Increased risk to core entity
Characteristics of supplier		Can select most innovative outsourcing organization
Country	Risk propensity varies by country	Outsourcing opportunities with low cost tend to be in riskier locations
Competitive risk	Need to differentiate products	Outsourced products available to competitors
Customer risk	Customer likelihood of placing orders; product obsolescence	Low-quality products may drive away customers Outsourcing may reduce the risk of product obsolescence
Downside risk	Risk of negative outcome (failure)	Outsourcing vendors can be replaced
Financial risk	Loss due to financial markets	Core entity less likely to be brought down by outsourcing vendor failure than by subordinate failure
Interaction	Communication coordination	Outsourcing vendors are more independent Outsourcing vendors can impose requirements for shared systems
Legal risk	Litigation exposure	Risk lower for core entity, as burden shifted to outsourcing vendor
Product risk	Product technical complexity	Core entities should make sure outsourcing organization is competent
Regulatory risk		Core entity risk lower, as outsourcing vendors assume local risk
Reputation risk	Customer confidence	Higher to core entities, as customers will hold core entities responsible
Shared risk		Outsourcing allows access to all potential vendors in the market
Supplier risk		Smaller organizations have greater risk
Supply disruption		If outsourcing supplier fails, that supplier can be replaced

Source: Cucchiella and Gastaldi (2006).[4]

Based on an example from Wu and Olson (2010),[5] we have seven vendors evaluated over 12 criteria. These criteria implicitly include risk in terms of business process procedures, source financial ability, technical capabilities, delivery performance record, and other criteria. I have selected components of Table 4.2 involving outsourcing risk and selected some that could reflect a given source selection decision in Table 4.3.

Table 4.3. Source Selection Criteria

Top level	Second level	Third level
Value	Quality	1. Supplier performance risk 2. Product quality 3. Customer perception of product 4. Product technical complexity
	Price	5. Risk propensity of supplier country 6. Competitive risk 7. Source financial risk
	Performance	8. Communication coordination 9. Legal/regulatory risk 10. Risk of supply disruption
	Facilities/ capabilities	11. Source utilization of assets 12. Source innovation ability

The next step is to apply swing weighting to obtain relative weight values, as in Table 4.4.

Table 4.4. Development of Swing Weights

Criteria	Swing weighting value	Divided by total
W2	100	0.182
W1	85	0.155
W3	75	0.136
W4	60	0.109
W5	50	0.091
W6	45	0.082
W7	40	0.073
W8	30	0.055
W9	25	0.045
W10	20	0.036
W11	15	0.027
W12	5	0.009
Total	550	1.000

Table 4.5 gives assessment data for the seven firms over these 12 criteria. Entries range from 0 (for worst possible performance) to 1.0 (for best possible performance).

Table 4.5. Vendor Alternative Scores

Category	Attribute	Vendor 1	Vendor 2	Vendor 3	Vendor 4	Vendor 5	Vendor 6	Vendor 7
A1 quality	Performance	0.82	0.90	0.78	0.95	0.75	0.70	0.75
A2 quality	Product	0.88	0.85	0.90	0.75	0.82	0.90	0.78
A3 quality	Perception	0.83	0.70	0.75	0.85	0.85	0.90	0.90
A4 quality	Complexity	0.88	0.75	0.85	0.70	0.80	0.85	0.82
A5 price	Country	0.88	0.95	0.78	0.80	0.85	0.90	0.85
A6 price	Competition	0.78	0.68	0.80	0.80	0.78	0.80	0.83
A7 price	Financial	0.92	0.74	0.85	0.78	0.90	0.75	0.70
A8 performance	Coordination	0.80	0.90	0.60	1.00	0.80	0.78	0.82
A9 performance	Legal	0.75	0.73	0.85	0.70	0.70	0.85	0.80
A10 performance	Disruption	0.55	0.78	0.65	0.75	0.78	0.68	0.76
A11 facilities	Assets	0.80	0.78	0.65	0.55	0.80	0.83	0.78
A12 facilities	Innovation	0.83	0.90	0.95	1.00	0.77	0.79	0.70

The value of each source alternative is calculated as in Table 4.6.

In this case, Vendor 1 had the highest score, slightly ahead of Vendor 6. Table 4.6 shows where Vendor 1 has relative advantages and disadvantages. This vendor was rated higher than any other source on A4 Product Technical Complexity and A7 Source Financial Risk. Its weakest rating was for A10 Risk of Supply Disruption, but that was compensated for by relatively strong ratings on other criteria. Vendor 6 was very close, with relatively high ratings on A2 Product Quality, A3 Customer Perceptions of Product, A5 Risk in Supplier Country, A9 Legal/Regulatory Risk, and A11 Source Asset Utilization. V6 was relatively weak on A1 Supplier Performance Risk, A7 Source Financial Risk, A8 Communication Coordination, and A10 Risk of Supply Disruption. These data can be used in value analysis to improve each source to make it more competitive. But for the current situation, the value function developed would recommend Vendor 1.

Table 4.6. Value Score Calculation

	Weights	Vendor 1	Vendor 2	Vendor 3	Vendor 4	Vendor 5	Vendor 6	Vendor 7
A1 performance	0.155	0.82	0.90	0.78	0.95	0.75	0.70	0.75
A2 product	0.182	0.88	0.85	0.90	0.75	0.82	0.90	0.78
A3 perception	0.136	0.83	0.70	0.75	0.85	0.85	0.90	0.90
A4 complexity	0.109	0.88	0.75	0.85	0.70	0.80	0.85	0.82
A5 country	0.091	0.88	0.95	0.78	0.80	0.85	0.90	0.85
A6 competition	0.082	0.78	0.68	0.80	0.80	0.78	0.80	0.83
A7 financial	0.073	0.92	0.74	0.85	0.78	0.90	0.75	0.70
A8 coordination	0.055	0.80	0.90	0.60	1.00	0.80	0.78	0.82
A9 legal	0.045	0.75	0.73	0.85	0.70	0.70	0.85	0.80
A10 disruption	0.036	0.55	0.78	0.65	0.75	0.78	0.68	0.76
A11 assets	0.027	0.80	0.78	0.65	0.55	0.80	0.83	0.78
A12 innovation	0.009	0.83	0.90	0.95	1.00	0.77	0.79	0.70
Value score		0.834	0.807	0.799	0.808	0.807	0.825	0.802

Supplier Management Process[6]

The growth of global supply chains has made supplier selection more involved, and long term. The overall process includes supplier selection, segmentation into groups with similar characteristics, and actively managing suppliers for long-term advantage to both parties. Supplier segments can be used to identify the potential suppliers for specific items. The supplier segmentation process involves steps of:

1. Identifying key features of customer segments
2. Identification of critical supplier characteristics
3. Selection of relevant variables for supplier segmentation
4. Identification of supplier segments

Different studies have used a variety of variables as the basis for classifying supplies into categories, much like ABC analysis. In supply chain management, if variables risk and profit impact were used, categories might be:

- **Noncritical** items with low risk and low profit impact
- **Leverage** items with low risk and high profit impact
- **Bottleneck** items with high risk and low profit impact
- **Strategic** items with high risk and high profit impact

Many other variables have been identified as potentially important in supplier management. Basic operational factors include delivery performance, quality, and warranty performance in addition to risk and profit. Process factors can include reserve capacity as well as supplier process capability and labor relations history. Green factors can include hazardous waste management, pollution reduction capability, and hazardous emissions management. Segmenting suppliers can be used as a basis for supplier selection for specific items, as well as a strategic tool to assist suppliers in improving their performance.

Rezaei and Ortt illustrated the concept of supplier segmentation management in a food company. This industry involves fast-changing demand of many perishable items with quality variable across suppliers. Delivery reliability is also an important factor. The company studied was in the chicken broiler industry, buying newly hatched chicks as well as fodder, medication, and equipment from 43 different suppliers. They raised chicks to marketable weight at which time they sold them. Suppliers were evaluated on capability (six criteria) and willingness to cooperate (six criteria) shown in Table 4.7.

Table 4.7. Supplier Segmentation Criteria by Category

Capability-related	Willingness-related
Price	Commitment to quality
Delivery reliability	Communication openness
Quality	Reciprocity
Reserve capacity	Willingness to share information
Geographical location	Supplier just-in-time efforts
Financial position	Willingness to form long-term relationship

The conceptual framework for supplier selection began with identifying the importance of functions for a specific item. Criteria from Table 4.7 would be rank ordered by importance. Then suppliers would be selected from among those of the 43 suppliers who offered the items in question. These suppliers are then segmented into the four categories described above (noncritical, leverage, bottleneck, strategic). The management phase of the process would be to determine a suitable strategy for each segment. Score sheets were used to assess each supplier on each of the 12 criteria using a 1 (very low) to 5 (very high) score. The results were used to categorize each segment. Those suppliers with low capabilities and low willingness were one segment (SM1). Those with low capabilities but high willingness were SM2. Those with high capabilities but low willingness were assigned SM3. Those with high capabilities as well as high willingness were SM4. When a specific item was needed, suppliers offering that item were assessed, and if lacking in capability or willingness, ways of improving that supplier's assessments were sought. If not, alternative suppliers were sought. If no adequate supplier was identified, the company sought to perform needed functions internally.

Specifically, eight suppliers provided marketing and sales services, delivered raised chickens to processing plants, and sold finished products to fastfood or other restaurants and to retailers. In this case, management considered price, geographical location, market knowledge, and financial position to be important capabilities, with willingness criteria of honest and frequent communication, willingness to share information, and long-term relationship. The final product had very high storage costs. Score sheets were used to assess potential suppliers on the 1–5 scale mentioned above. Capabilities and willingness were equally rated and averaged, identifying no suppliers in SM1, one supplier in SM2, one in SM3, and six in SM4. The outcome of the analysis can be two-fold: first, the six suppliers in SM4 could be evaluated more closely to make specific purchase decisions. In fact, continuous scores enabled differentiation among these suppliers to enable the identification of a specific preferred supplier. But those in lower categories could be worked with to improve their scores, making them better partners for future transactions.

This approach is parallel to multiple criteria analysis as described in the SMART technique. Rezaei and Ortt didn't spend much time on relative weights, but the scoring is directly parallel to that of SMART. For specific sourcing decisions (picking a supplier for a specific item), the input provided by Rezaei and Ortt could be used, supplemented by swing weighting, to obtain recommendations for each case.

A feature of the Rezaei and Ortt process that is very attractive is the focus on working with suppliers to improve and to develop long-range relationships.

Product Design Selection

Barker, T. J., & Zabinsky, Z. B. (2011). A multicriteria decision making model for reverse logistics using analytical hierarchy process. *Omega*, *39*(5), 558–573.

Another important supply chain decision involves aspects of product design. Contemporary operations need to consider environmental considerations, including recycling, refurbishing, and reuse.[7] Companies need to decide how to collect recoverable products, how to separate recoverable resources from useless scrap, where to reprocess recoverable products to make them marketable, and how to distribute recovered products to future customers. In Barker and Zabinsky (2011), three examples are given: recycling a medical device, recycling residential carpet, and recycling commercial carpet. The options given as available consist of three binary options:

1. Collection could be proprietary or industry wide.
2. Sorting and testing material collected could be centralized or distributed.
3. Processing of recovered material could be at the original facility or at a secondary facility.

Thus there are eight combinations of these three binary options. Criteria considered were costs (consisting of recycled product costs, testing costs, shipping costs for scrap, and original production costs), proprietary knowledge involved, and impact on customer interaction. Proprietary knowledge considerations focused on the degree to which the producer wanted to keep return products out of competitor hands. Customer relationships dealt with warranty and guarantee matters.

The SMART model begins by ranking the three criteria in the context of the given recycling product. For recycling a medical device, we might rank proprietary knowledge first, cost second, and customer relations third. Then, swing weighting needs to be applied. A rating of 100 is given to the swing from the worst to the best case of proprietary knowledge, a rating of 60 is given to the swing from the worst to the best case for cost, and a rating of 30 is given to the swing from the worst to the best case for customer relations. This totals 190. Dividing each rating by 190 yields relative weights of 0.526 for proprietary considerations, 0.316 for cost, and 0.158 for customer relations.

What is next required is a set of scores for the alternatives for a decision context. Table 4.8 gives relative scores for the eight configurations for recycling a medical device, along with value calculations.

In this case, the proprietary, decentralized operation at the original facility is recommended, with the proprietary, centralized operation at the original facility a close second. Keeping operations in-house has the advantage of controlling proprietary knowledge of the product.

The second example is for recycling residential carpet. The weights of criteria would change, with a possible ranking of cost as the most important criterion, followed by customer relations and proprietary considerations. If cost is assigned a swing rating of 100, customer relations might be 80 and proprietary considerations 40. This would yield relative weights of 0.455 for cost, 0.364 for customer relations, and 0.182 for proprietary knowledge. The scores might change with the context as well, as shown in Table 4.9.

Table 4.8. Medical Device Recycling Value Calculation

Configuration	Cost	Pro-prietary	Relations	Value
Weights	0.316	0.526	0.158	
Proprietary, centralized, original facility	0.70	1.00	0.65	0.850
Proprietary, centralized, secondary facility	0.30	0.95	0.75	0.713
Proprietary, decentralized, original facility	0.85	0.90	0.80	**0.868**
Proprietary, decentralized, secondary facility	0.40	0.70	0.70	0.605
Industry-wide, centralized, original facility	0.60	0.50	0.80	0.579
Industry-wide, centralized, secondary facility	0.50	0.30	0.90	0.458
Industry-wide, decentralized, original facility	0.65	0.40	1.00	0.574
Industry-wide, decentralized, secondary facility	0.45	0.20	0.95	0.398

Table 4.9. Residential Carpet Recycling Value Calculation

Configuration	Cost	Pro-prietary	Relations	Value
Weights	0.455	0.182	0.364	
Proprietary, centralized, original facility	0.50	1.00	0.40	0.555
Proprietary, centralized, secondary facility	0.30	0.95	0.60	0.528
Proprietary, decentralized, original facility	0.55	0.85	0.70	0.660
Proprietary, decentralized, secondary facility	0.50	0.80	0.70	0.628
Industry-wide, centralized, original facility	0.40	0.60	0.85	0.601
Industry-wide, centralized, secondary facility	0.50	0.50	0.90	0.646
Industry-wide, decentralized, original facility	0.65	0.30	1.00	0.714
Industry-wide, decentralized, secondary facility	0.85	0.20	0.95	**0.769**

In this case, the analysis recommends an industry-wide, decentralized approach using a secondary facility. The same solution using the original facility would be the next recommended alternative.

For recycling of commercial carpet, again, a different set of weights might apply. If cost is ranked first, followed by proprietary knowledge and then customer relations, and if swing weights of 100 for cost, 60 for proprietary considerations, and 20 for customer relations are applied, the relative weights would be 0.555 for cost, 0.333 for proprietary knowledge, and 0.111 for customer relations. Table 4.10 provides value calculations in this case.

Here the new weights and scores yield a recommended option of proprietary, decentralized operations in the original facility.

IBM Decision Support System

Kirkwood, C. W., Slaven, M. P., & Maltz, A. (2005). Improving supply-chain-reconfiguration decisions at IBM. *Interfaces*, *35*(6), 460–473.

IBM has many midlevel supply chain decisions, including make-or-buy decisions, regional sourcing, and decisions involving location and logistics.

Table 4.10. Commercial Carpet Recycling Value Calculation

Configuration	Cost	Proprietary	Relations	Value
Weights	0.555	0.333	0.111	
Proprietary, centralized, original facility	0.60	1.00	0.40	0.710
Proprietary, centralized, secondary facility	0.40	0.95	0.60	0.605
Proprietary, decentralized, original facility	0.70	0.85	0.70	**0.749**
Proprietary, decentralized, secondary facility	0.65	0.80	0.70	0.705
Industry-wide, centralized, original facility	0.50	0.50	0.85	0.538
Industry-wide, centralized, secondary facility	0.30	0.40	0.90	0.400
Industry-wide, decentralized, original facility	0.65	0.20	1.00	0.538
Industry-wide, decentralized, secondary facility	0.75	0.10	0.95	0.555

Global operations increasingly take advantage of global manufacturing sources to gain cost efficiencies, to broaden their geographical supply base, and to increase procurement options. A decision support system (DSS) was developed to support these critical supply chain decisions.[8]

Prior to applying the DSS, the process to evaluate sourcing for manufacturing involved the following steps:

1. Study, identification, and evaluation
2. Decision
3. Execution and communication

A DSS was developed to aid in the first step. IBM policy specified that this step should include

- identification of optimization possibilities;
- specification of sourcing considerations;
- analysis of financial and nonfinancial issues;
- assessment of supplier risks;
- assessment of risk ranges and rewards for IBM; and
- make-or-buy decision.

The supply chain DSS was to consider financial and nonfinancial considerations and their trade-offs, as well as uncertainties. A general list of evaluation considerations was developed, as shown in Table 4.11.

Scoring systems were created to measure each of these defined considerations. Costs were assessed using expert judgment. A utility function was developed to obtain weights through interviews with IBM analysts and managers. Swing weighting was applied, assuming that weights should be similar across decisions.

The DSS supported sensitivity analysis by expediting changes in weights and scores. The model extended beyond what I have described in this chapter to include probability analysis. The DSS was developed on Excel. The system was tested on five IBM supply chain reconfiguration decisions:

- the make-or-buy decision between internal IBM production and a contractor;

Table 4.11. IBM Supply Chain Configuration Evaluation Considerations

Consideration	Definition
Cost	
Manufacturing value-added	Volume, labor, facility development, and other expenses
Outbound transportation to customer	Freight to deliver goods to customers
Inbound transportation	Freight from supplier to IBM facility
Launch cost	Supply chain control costs
Inventory carrying cost	Finance charge
Taxes	Corporate taxes on profits and royalty income
One-time transition cost	Costs to close facilities and cleanup
Quality	
Cost of quality	Decrease in net present value (NPV) for repair and warranty
Manufacturing process quality	Defects in manufacturing
Fulfillment and customer quality	Costs to improve customer satisfaction
Customer responsiveness	
Cycle time	Time from order to customer receipt
Missed commitments	Ability to meet on-time promises
Revenue recognition	Ability to meet prioritizations and order churn
Strategic	
Core competencies	Ability to outsource low complexity and retain products with significant intellectual property
Fixed versus variable costs	Lower fixed costs preferred
Effect on corporate tax	Overall after-tax corporate profit
Supply chain geopolitical risk	Transparency International Corruption Perceptions Index (CPI)
Financial	Cash-flow acceleration, inflation
Operations	
Physical infrastructure	Potential to utilize unused capacity
Sophistication and skills	Potential to utilize unused skills, training
Support structure	Additional effort needed to maintain relationship
Information technology and business process continuity	Extent of process interactions between IBM and source

- producing another product internally or through a contractor, with tax advantages a major factor;
- producing a third product at either U.S. IBM facilities or Asian IBM facilities;
- production of a fourth product at existing facilities or a new IBM location, preferred by the source; and
- production of a fifth product in either of two Asian countries.

The decisions were supported by the analysis of the criteria where relative advantages and disadvantages were found.

Conclusion

Supply chain operations include many contexts requiring decisions among available options. A key point is that decision makers do not have to settle for only those options immediately available. Value-focused risk analysis aims to support decision-maker generation of new and better alternatives. A value hierarchy demonstrates typical risks present in supply chain selection decisions. Once options are identified, the SMART technique can help sort out the trade-offs present when risk is involved, as was demonstrated in the source selection example. Real examples of product design selection and supply chain configuration were also described.

This chapter demonstrated how multiple criteria selection can be supported with a simple multiattribute rating technique. Two examples were given, demonstrating supply chain decisions involving multiple criteria. The first was to select a source; the second was to aid decisions involving product recycling. The SMART method is quite flexible, and risk can be an important aspect of scores assigned to alternatives being evaluated.

CHAPTER 5

Simulation of Supply Chain Risk

Supply chains involve many risks, as we have seen. Modeling those risks requires consideration of probability, which calls for Monte Carlo simulation, a well-developed analytic technique. This chapter shows two basic simulation models involving supply chains: a supply chain software business case and inventory modeling.

Monte Carlo Simulation

Simulation models are sets of assumptions concerning the relationships among model components. Simulations can be time oriented (for instance, involving the number of events such as demands in a day) or process oriented (for instance, involving queuing systems of arrivals and services). Uncertainty can be included by using probabilistic inputs for elements such as demands, interarrival times, or service times. These probabilistic inputs need to be described by probability distributions with specified parameters. Probability distributions can include normal distributions (parameters for mean and variance), exponential distributions (parameters for a mean), lognormal (parameters for mean and variance), or any of a number of other distributions. A simulation run is a sample from an infinite population of possible results for a given model. After a simulation model is built, the number of trials is established. Statistical methods are used to validate simulation models and design simulation experiments.

Many financial simulation models can be accomplished on spreadsheets, such as Excel. There are a number of commercial add-on products that can be added to Excel, such as @Risk, Frontline Solver, or Crystal Ball, that vastly extend the simulation power of spreadsheet models.[1] These add-ons make it very easy to replicate simulation runs and include the ability to correlate variables, expeditiously select from standard distributions, aggregate and display output, and other useful functions.

Supply Chain Risk Simulation[2]

Supply chain networks offer great cost advantages, but also have corresponding risks to trade-off. This book has discussed some of the many risks involved in global supply chains. These risks can arise from many sources, to include natural disaster, geopolitical failure, market failure, and industrial accidents. Some of these risks can be described in terms of probability distributions based on past statistics. Others require subjective assessment by people as expert as can be obtained. Monte Carlo simulation is a useful technique to model outcomes given inputs described probabilistically.

Klibi and Martel described a Canadian military planning environment where the Canadian supply network would be used to support overseas missions. Planning requires trade-off analysis between costs and support levels. Three major hazard categories were supported, to include disasters (met with by humanitarian assistance), quarrels (with peacekeeping response), and wars (with response of peace enforcement). Each of these hazards had distinct logistic support needs and vulnerabilities. The critical Canadian supply network resources were depots and vendors.

Supply Chain Network Hazard Modeling

Supply chain networks usually involve dispersion, often international, inherently involving risk. There is a need for robustness, capable of dealing with highly uncertain events. Historical data and classical statistics can provide some probability estimates, but many situations will need to rely on the judgmental estimates of probabilities and impacts. Klibi and Martel's system relies on the questions:

1. What can go wrong?
2. What are the consequences?
3. What are the likelihoods?

Some events are so highly uncertain that only the first two of these questions are appropriate. Others involve repetitive hazards, to include natural disasters, geopolitical failures, market failures, and industrial accidents. The approach involves the following phases:

- Characterize hazards and sources of vulnerability: (identify hazard zones, yielding vulnerabilities sources, hazard zones, and exposure levels)
- Model hazard processes: (describe hazards to specify intensity and duration)
- Model impact of events: (consider attenuation probabilities capable of dealing with adverse events, and recovery times)

One of the contexts used to demonstrate the methodology was that of the supply network for Canadian Forces. Canada's military needs to be able to respond to disasters (humanitarian assistance), quarrels (peacekeeping), and war. Logistics and supply chains were initially developed millennia ago to support such military activities.

Thus the hazard modeling approach would involve the development of analysis of the three fundamental questions given above for each mission in each area of operation. Key elements include mission **intensity**, which depends on **severity** (reflecting level of enemy aggression and the physical nature of theatre terrain) and **magnitude** (number of people deployed). Required logistic support is directly proportional to mission intensity.

Each mission involves three phases: **Deployment** is the period where troops are moved to the theater, and logistic support ensures that they have proper shelter and basic commodities upon arrival. **Sustainment** is the main mission phase. Supply during sustainment provides goods consumed during the mission. **Redeployment** occurs when missions are completed, with supply activities focusing on moving materiel back to Canada from the operating theater.

NATO forces have five basic classes of supply as follows:

- Class I—subsistence, consumed at a roughly uniform rate;
- Class II—supplies specified by tables of organization and equipment, such as clothing, weapons, tools, vehicles, and spare parts;
- Class III—fuels and lubricants;
- Class IV—usually fortification and construction materials;
- Class V—ammunition, explosives, etc.

The methodology involves identifying risks for each location and type of mission (disaster, peacekeeping, war) with associated probabilities and magnitudes, for each of class of supply over a time horizon of 10 years by week. The technique of modeling risk is to generate simulations for event occurrence, and given occurrence, simulation of magnitude and severity. Occurrence is a matter of probability, and can be obtained ideally based upon historical statistics, but often requiring subjective expert judgment. Magnitude and severity can be modeled by whatever distribution is deemed appropriate. Klibi and Martel demonstrated weekly pallet flows for a specific product family, but the methodology clearly can be applied to a massive number of contingent combinations. The value of the analysis is to show the potential strain on a logistic system, and provided the Canadian military with worst-case scenarios (the worst outcomes out of all simulation runs).

Net Present Value (NPV) Example

Consider a proposed advanced planning system implementation study conducted by a small team of company personnel, aided by a hired consultant. At this stage of the analysis, typically expected costs are underestimated, and there is some uncertainty with particular estimates. The analysis initially includes the internal team plus consultant support to conduct the analysis and plan the system, a business process reengineering study, and the formation of a training team. Hardware will be purchased over the first two years. The second year will involve acquisition of software and its installation (with an ongoing maintenance contract), additional acquisition of hardware, and increased training expense. Subsequent years will see lower internal team costs, but increasing training costs. Benefits from the system are not expected until the third year. The estimated costs by category are shown in Table 5.1. Probabilistic cells in Table 5.1 are indicated by the darker shading. The last cell in column I, marked with lighter shading, is an output measure (in this case, NPV). Crystal Ball software (as well as its competitors) provides an easy method to include probability distributions and measures of selected results.

This model applies NPV analysis. The first year, following conventional accounting practice, is considered year 0, and costs that year are treated as occurring immediately. The NPV is obtained by taking benefits minus all expenses for each time period (in this case year) and dividing each row's value by 1 plus the discount rate. Here we assume a cost of capital of 20%, so the discount is 1.2. Discounting is compounded, so the year (column A) is an exponent for the discount rate, as shown in

Table 5.1. Advanced Planning System Costs

A	B	C	D	E	F	G	H	I
Year	Internal team	Cons	Software	Hardware	Training	Benefit	Net	Discount (20%)
0	500,000	600,000	0	500,000	200,000	0	=G2-$\sum$(B2:F2)	=H2/(1.2^A2)
1	700,000	1,200,000	8,000,000	1,500,000	500,000	0	=G3-$\sum$(B3:F3)	=H3/(1.2^A3)
2	300,000	0	1,000,000	0	300,000	5,000,000	=G4-$\sum$(B4:F4)	=H4/(1.2^A4)
3	200,000	0	1,000,000	0	300,000	7,000,000	=G5-$\sum$(B5:F5)	=H5/(1.2^A5)
4	200,000	0	1,000,000	0	300,000	11,000,000	=G6-$\sum$(B6:F6)	=H6/(1.2^A6)
5	200,000	0	1,000,000	0	300,000	14,000,000	=G7-$\sum$(B7:F7)	=H7/(1.2^A7)
								=SUM(I2:I7)

column I. The NPV is the sum of all rows in column I. This provides the current value of the entire project over the time horizon analyzed (in this case, 6 total years).

Some of these estimates are considered highly variable. Monte Carlo simulation allows the use of distributions to reflect these inputs.[3] There are a number of distributions available. In this case, consultant expenses are considered to follow the uniform distribution, defined as a range of equally probable values. For year 0, consultant expense is estimated to be uniformly distributed between a minimum of $400,000 and a maximum of $800,000, and for year 1, a minimum of $1,000,000 and a maximum of $1,400,000.

Training expenses in the first year involve organization of training and can be budgeted in a controlled manner. However, implementation of training in subsequent years will involve high levels of uncertainty. In year 1, these expenses are expected to follow a triangular distribution, with a minimum of $400,000, a most likely value of $500,000, and a maximum of $700,000. For subsequent years this expense is expected to continue as new employees appear, but there is a much wider range of possibilities:

Year 2, minimum $250,000, most likely $300,000, maximum $450,000
Year 3, minimum $200,000, most likely $300,000, maximum $500,000
Year 4, minimum $150,000, most likely $300,000, maximum $600,000
Year 5, minimum $100,000, most likely $300,000, maximum $700,000

Benefits are the most unpredictable numbers in the analysis. They also take some time to develop. The normal distribution is assumed, with the following parameters:

Year 2, mean $5,000,000, standard deviation $1,000,000
Year 3, mean $7,000,000, standard deviation $1,500,000
Year 4, mean $11,000,000, standard deviation $2,000,000
Year 5, mean $14,000,000, standard deviation $3,000,000

Crystal Ball provides an easy means to input these probabilistic inputs into an Excel spreadsheet and also provides an easy means to run the model and display the results of the NPV (the last cell in column I). The simulation is run as many times as the user specifies (within limits—up to 10,000). Here the model was run 1,000 times, and Crystal Ball collected statistics on NPV. The statistics for this model were

Trials	1,000
Mean	$3,276,370
Median	$3,262,163
Standard deviation	$1,891,684
Minimum	-$2,649,315
Maximum	$9,864,451

A histogram of this cell is shown in Figure 5.1.

Crystal Ball also provides a means to identify the proportion of cases between selected ranges. Here we are interested in the probability of losing money on the proposed advanced planning system. We selected a minimum level of 0, and Crystal Ball returns a certainty level of 95.86 in Figure 5.1, indicating that 959 times out of 1,000 the NPV was positive. (That also implies a probability of 0.042 of benefits not covering costs—a clear indicator of project risk.)

Inventory Systems

Inventory is any resource that is set aside for future use. Inventory is necessary because the demand and supply of goods usually are not perfectly matched at any given time or place. Supply chains involve many inventories between elements. The more inventory retained on hand, the less likelihood of running out. However, inventory has costs. Lean manufacturing systems are designed on the premise that inventory is a very

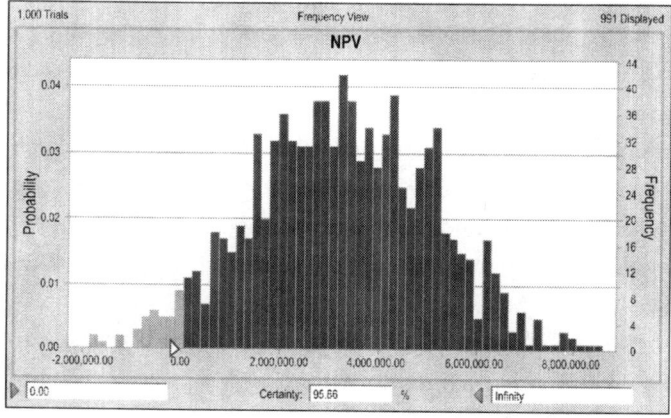

Figure 5.1. Histogram of the Advanced Planning System NPV

bad thing and should be eliminated if possible. However, few operations, including supply chains, have the level of predictability needed to make such a system possible.

The basic risks associated with inventories are the risk of running out of stock (and thus losing sales) and the counterrisk of going broke because excessive cash flow is tied up in inventory. The problem is made interesting because demand is almost always uncertain, driven by the behavior of the market—usually many people making spontaneous purchasing decisions.

The two basic inventory decisions that managers face are *how much* to order or produce and *when* to order or produce it. Although it is possible to consider these two decisions separately, they are so closely related that a simultaneous solution is usually necessary. Typically the objective is to minimize total inventory costs.

Total inventory costs include four components: holding costs, ordering costs, shortage costs, and purchasing costs. **Holding costs**, or **carrying costs**, represent costs associated with maintaining inventory. These costs include interest incurred or the opportunity cost of having capital tied up in inventory; storage costs such as insurance, taxes, rental fees, utilities, and other maintenance costs for storage space; warehousing or storage operation costs, including handling, record keeping, information processing, and actual physical inventory expenses; and costs associated with deterioration, shrinkage, obsolescence, and damage. Total holding costs are dependent on how many items are stored and for how long. Therefore, holding costs are expressed in terms of dollars associated with carrying one unit of inventory for one unit of time.

Ordering costs represent costs associated with replenishing inventories. These costs are not dependent on how many items are ordered at a time, but on the number of orders that are prepared. Ordering costs include overhead, clerical work, data processing, and other expenses that are incurred in searching for supply sources, as well as costs associated with purchasing, expediting, transporting, receiving, and inspecting. Ordering costs are constant and are expressed in terms of dollars per order.

Shortage costs, or **stock-out costs**, are those costs that occur when demand exceeds available inventory in stock. A shortage may be handled as a *backorder*, in which a customer waits until the item is available, or as a *lost sale*. In either case, a shortage represents lost profit and possible loss of future sales. Shortage costs depend on how much shortage has occurred and, sometimes, for how long. Shortage costs are expressed in terms of dollar cost per unit of the item.

Purchasing costs are what firms pay for the materials or goods. In most inventory models, the price of materials is the same regardless of the quantity purchased; in this case, purchasing costs can be ignored. However, when price varies by quantity purchased, called a *quantity discount*, inventory analysis must be adjusted to account for this difference.

Basic Inventory Simulation Model

Many models contain variables that change continuously over time. One example would be a model of a retail store's inventory. The number of items changes gradually (though discretely) over an extended time period; however, for all intents and purposes, they may be treated as continuous. As customer demand is fulfilled, inventory is depleted, leading to factory orders to replenish the stock. As orders are received from suppliers, inventory increases. Over time, particularly if orders are relatively small and frequent as we see in just-in-time environments, the inventory level can be represented by a smooth, continuous function.

We can build a simple inventory simulation model beginning with a spreadsheet model as shown in Table 5.1. Model parameters include a holding rate of 0.8 per item per day, an order rate of 300 for each order placed, a purchase price of 90, and a sales price of 130. The decision variables are when to order (when the end-of-day quantity drops below the reorder point [ROP]) and the quantity to order (Q). The model itself has a row for each day (here 30 days are modeled). Each day has a starting inventory (column B) and a probabilistic demand (column C) generated from a normal distribution with a mean of 100 and a standard deviation of 10. Demand is an integer. Sales (column D) are equal to the minimum of the starting quantity and demand. End-of-day inventory (column E) is the maximum of 0 or the starting inventory minus demand. The quantity ordered at the end of each day in column F (here assumed to be on hand at the beginning of the next day) is 0 if ending inventory exceeds ROP, or Q if ending inventory drops to or below the ROP.

Initial model parameters are entered in cell B1 for holding cost rate (dollars per ending inventory item per day), B2 for order cost rate (dollars per order), B3 for purchase price (dollars per unit), and B4 for selling price (dollars per unit). The ROP policy is entered in cell E1, and the Q policy is entered in cell E2. Profit and shortage are calculated to the right of the basic inventory model. Column G calculates the holding cost by multiplying the parameter in cell B2 by the ending inventory quantity for each day, and summing over the 30 days in cell G5. Order costs are calculated by day as $200 if an order is placed that day and 0 otherwise, with the monthly total ordering cost accumulated in cell H5. Cell I5 calculates the total purchasing cost, cell J5 calculates total revenue, and cell H3 calculates net profit considering the value of the starting inventory and ending inventory. Column K (not shown in Table 5.2) identifies sales lost (SHORT), with cell K5 accumulating these for the month. The formulas for the recursive inventory model are shown in Table 5.2.

Table 5.2. Formulas for the Inventory Model

Column	Definition	Formula row 7	Formula row 8
A	Day (count)	=1	=A7+1
B	Start inventory	=20	=E7+F7
C	Demand	=INT(CB. Exponential(0.2,1)+.5)	=INT(CB. Exponential(0.2,1)+.5)
D	Sales	=MIN(B7,C7)	=MIN(B7,C7)
E	End inventory	=B7-D7	=B7-D7
F	Order	=IF(E7<=$E$1,$E$2,0)	=IF(E7<=$E$1,$E$2,0)
G	Hold cost	+$B$1*E7	+$B$1*E7
H	Order cost	=IF F7 > 0,$B$2,0)	=IF F7 > 0,$B$2,0)
I	Purchase	=$B$3*F7	=$B$3*F7
J	Revenue	=$B$4*D7	=$B$4*D7
K	Short	=IF(C7 > B7,C7-B7,0)	=IF(C7 > B7,C7-B7,0)

Table 5.3 shows the Excel spreadsheet with Crystal Ball entries shaded.

Table 5.3. Crystal Ball Basic Inventory Model

A	B	C	D	E	F	G	H	I	J
1 Hold rate	2		ROP	60					
2 Order rate	200		Q	60					
3 Purchase	150					Net	270		
4 Sell	200							1500	
5						3,280	400	18,000	15,800
6 Day	Start	Demand	Sales	End	Order	Hold cost	Order cost	Purchase	Revenue
7 1	20	3	3	17	60	34	200	9,000	600
8 2	77	4	4	73	0	146	0	0	800
9 3	73	6	6	67	0	134	0	0	1,200
10 4	67	4	4	63	0	126	0	0	800
11 5	63	3	3	60	60	120	200	9,000	600
12 6	120	3	3	117	0	234	0	0	600
13 7	117	2	2	115	0	230	0	0	400
14 8	115	4	4	111	0	222	0	0	800
15 9	111	4	4	107	0	214	0	0	800
16 10	107	6	6	101	0	202	0	0	1,200
17 11	101	3	3	98	0	196	0	0	600
18 12	98	2	2	96	0	192	0	0	400
19 13	96	3	3	93	0	186	0	0	600
20 14	93	2	2	91	0	182	0	0	400
21 15	91	6	6	85	0	170	0	0	1,200
22 16	85	6	6	79	0	158	0	0	1,200
23 17	79	7	7	72	0	144	0	0	1,400
24 18	72	3	3	69	0	138	0	0	600
25 19	69	4	4	65	0	130	0	0	800
26 20	65	4	4	61	0	122	0	0	800

Crystal Ball simulation software allows the introduction of three types of special variables. Probabilistic variables (assumption cells in Crystal Ball terminology) are modeled in column C using a normal distribution (CB.Normal(mean, std)). Decision variables are modeled in Table 5.3 for ROP (cell E1) and Q (cell E2) as described previously as policy parameters. Crystal Ball allows setting minimum and maximum levels for decision variables, as well as step size. Here we used ROP values of 30, 40, 50, and 60, and Q values of 30, 40, 50, and 60. The third type of variable is a forecast cell. We have forecast cells for net profit (cell H3) and for sales lost (cell K3).

The Crystal Ball simulation can be set to run for up to 10,000 repetitions for combinations of decision variables. We selected 1,000 repetitions. Output is provided for the forecast cells. Figure 5.2 shows net profit for the combination of an ROP of 60 and a Q of 60.

The interesting series of hills shown in Figure 5.2 come from clusters of output for different events. Most of the results cluster around profitability for the month slightly below $2,000. This group of results experienced few stock-outs. There is another cluster around a monthly loss of $6,000, when more stock-outs were experienced. Figure 5.2 demonstrates some value provided by the Crystal Ball output of the inventory

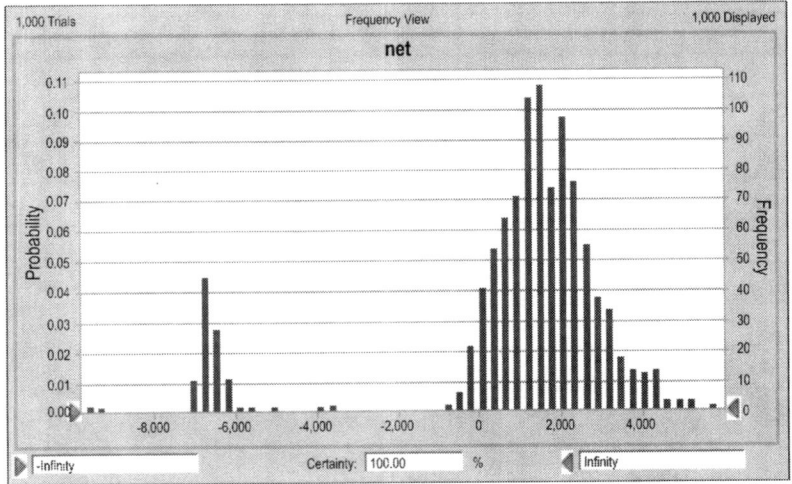

Figure 5.2. Crystal Ball Output for Net Profit for ROP 60, Q 60

model. The statistics in tabular form are shown in Table 5.4. There was a mean profit of $1,000 per month; the minimum was a loss of more than $9,500 (the maximum was a gain of $5,760).

Table 5.4. Statistical Output for Net Profit for ROP 60, Q 60

Statistic	Net profit	Stock-outs
Mean	999.81	2.38
Median	1,605.00	0.00
Mode	2,446.00	0.00
Standard deviation	2,711.28	4.52
Minimum	−9,582.00	0.00
Maximum	5,760.00	28.00

The histogram for the forecast variable SHORT is shown in Figure 5.3. This histogram enables identification of the probability of shortage over a month (in this case $1 - 0.4085 = 0.59$).

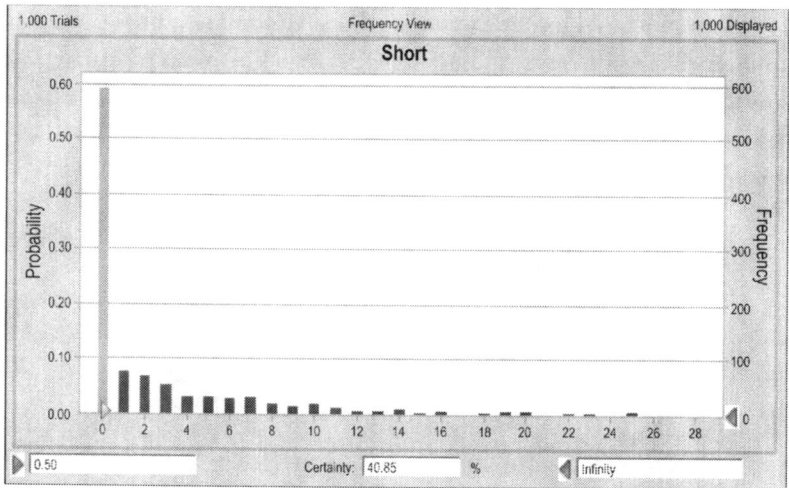

Figure 5.3. SHORT for ROP 60, Q 60

Crystal Ball also provides the ability to obtain a comparison over all decision variable values. This requires modeling ROP in cell E1 and Q in cell E2 as decision variables and using the modeling tool *Decision Table*. Here both ROP and Q were set to be discrete variables with a minimum of 30, a maximum of 60, and a step size of 10. Crystal Ball ran the inventory model 12 times, with 1,000 runs each, generating the output in Figure 5.4 (different results from Table 5.4 are due to random numbers).

	Q (30.00)	Q (40.00)	Q (50.00)	Q (60.00)	
ROP (30.00)	2,346.76	2,568.24	2,674.44	1.943.84	1
ROP (40.00)	2,326.56	2,185.04	2,393.04	2,289.44	2
ROP (50.00)	1,760.16	1,749.84	1,315.04	1,914.24	3
ROP (60.00)	1,121.36	1,493.84	1,347.04	1,357.04	4
	1	2	3	4	

Figure 5.4. Comparative Net Profit for Step Values of ROP and Q

The implication here is that the best decision for the basic model parameters would be an ROP of 30 and a Q of 50, yielding an expected net profit of $2,674 for the month for this product. The shortage for this combination had a mean of 2.41 items per day. The mean probability of shortage was again 0.59. The combinations of ROP and Q used in Figure 5.4 are quite rough. It is good to focus, using a smaller grid. This was done, yielding the output in Figure 5.5.

	Q (47.00)	Q (48.00)	Q (49.00)	Q (50.00)	Q (51.00)	Q (52.00)	Q (53.00)	
ROP (10.00)	3,535.08	3,355.78	3,483.80	3,355.80	3,307.74	2,877.18	2,602.38	1
ROP (11.00)	3,365.70	3,556.50	3,373.36	3,487.52	3,295.46	3,011.12	2,744.96	2
ROP (12.00)	3,192.78	3,454.50	3,287.84	3,391.64	3,283.42	3,067.42	2,715.32	3
ROP (13.00)	3,025.38	3,504.22	3,552.26	3,149.50	3,414.12	3,140.44	2,764.14	4
ROP (14.00)	3,131.58	3,102.06	3,370.20	3,348.68	3,241.16	3,279.80	2,980.00	5
ROP (15.00)	3,107.40	2,993.24	3,341.80	3,396.80	3,134.18	3,103.28	2,972.16	6
ROP (16.00)	3,068.56	3,042.92	3,224.18	3,355.48	3,182.96	3,227.20	3,037.10	7
ROP (17.00)	3,108.28	2,939.34	2,898.86	3,238.48	3,378.84	3,043.46	3,165.48	8
	1	2	3	4	5	6	7	

Figure 5.5. Finer Grid of Net Profit for ROP, Q

Here the implication is that the highest net profit would be obtained with an ROP of 11 and a Q of 48. One of the features of simulation is that the results depend upon the random numbers drawn. Rerunning the simulation is likely to yield a different set of results. Here an ROP of 13 and a Q of 49 had a profit nearly as high, and the combination of an ROP of 10 and a Q of 47 was also high. That is a feature typically found in inventory simulations—a flat response surface, meaning that being precisely right doesn't matter that much. The stock-out results for this grid of ROP and Q are shown in Figure 5.6.

	Q (47.00)	Q (48.00)	Q (49.00)	Q (50.00)	Q (51.00)	Q (52.00)	Q (53.00)	
Trend Chart								
Overlay Chart								
Forecast Chart								
ROP (10.00)	3.21	3.40	3.52	3.34	3.62	4.00	3.81	1
ROP (11.00)	3.10	2.99	3.37	3.25	3.24	3.62	3.71	2
ROP (12.00)	2.93	2.90	2.77	3.14	2.95	3.37	3.54	3
ROP (13.00)	2.77	2.73	2.69	2.78	2.91	2.93	3.33	4
ROP (14.00)	2.77	2.66	2.61	2.54	2.66	2.72	3.17	5
ROP (15.00)	2.62	2.58	2.52	2.51	2.54	2.48	2.82	6
ROP (16.00)	2.56	2.45	2.50	2.45	2.37	2.48	2.39	7
ROP (17.00)	2.50	2.41	2.34	2.45	2.37	2.41	2.39	8
	1	2	3	4	5	6	7	

Figure 5.6. Stock-out for ROP, Q Combinations

It can be seen that the combination of an ROP of 10 and a Q of 47, which had a high net profit, has more risk of stock-outs. The combination of an ROP of 13 and a Q of 49 is better at 2.69 stock-outs. Of course, a higher Q and a higher ROP will reduce stock-outs, but at greater cost in other areas.

Conclusion

Supply chains involve quite a few risks balanced against their benefits in accessing lower-cost sources. When these risks can be quantified, Monte Carlo simulation provides a flexible and useful tool for analysis. Simulation models allow any assumption to be made, although the more that is assumed, the more complex the model becomes. In this chapter, two typical supply chain decisions were modeled with simulation. Financial evaluations of software systems are critically important to supply chains. An NPV analysis including risk for an advanced planning system was demonstrated. Inventory management is very important across supply chains, both in manufacturing and in retail environments. The trade-off between expected cost minimization and stock-out risk was demonstrated.

Overall, the value of simulation is the ability to make whatever assumptions are considered appropriate with respect to input parameters. Monte Carlo simulation is especially attractive when probability distributions are available for inputs. Crystal Ball (as well as @Risk and Frontline Solver) supports output analysis as well.

CHAPTER 6

Supply Chain Management Risk Models

Risk management has provided many tools to evaluate the chance of loss. Risk management has been defined as the identification, assessment, and prioritization of risks followed by coordinated and economical application of resources to minimize, monitor, and control the probability and impact of unfortunate events.[1] This is a comprehensive view of risk management, covering all possible risks facing an organization. The fact is that one cannot expect compensation or profit without taking on some risk. The key to successful risk management is to select those risks that one is competent to deal with and to find some way to avoid, reduce, or insure against the others.

Supply Chain Risk Model

Outsourcing reduces many risks to core organizations. Outsourcing can reduce financial exposure and may enable overcoming productive capacity limits of the core organization. Outsourcing can also make compliance with local regulations easier, may improve reaction to market timing, and may provide greater agility. Outsourcing organizations can also avoid many legal problems in their home countries.

I will demonstrate Monte Carlo simulation in supporting risk management using a scenario involving the selection of outsourcing supply vendors. I consider 12 available alternatives for delivery of a small product component located in different countries or the United States. These outsourcing options have expected characteristics over a number of features. I will demonstrate how simulation can be used to better understand uncertainties involved in price (and vendor survival probabilities). I will demonstrate how multiple criteria analysis can be used to focus on multiple aspects of decision problems, and how trade-off analysis can be used to rationally select preferred options. Note that the data used are purely hypothetical and do not imply relative performance for specific organizations in any country.

In supply chain outsourcing decisions, a number of factors can involve uncertainty, and simulation can be useful in gaining a better understanding of systems. I begin by looking at expected distributions of prices for the component to be outsourced from each location. China, in this case, has the lowest estimated prices, but it has a wide expected distribution of exchange rate fluctuation. These distributions will affect the actual realized price for the outsourced component. The Chinese vendors are also rated as having relatively high probabilities of failure in product compliance with contractual standards, in vendor financial survival, and in political stability of the host country. The simulation is modeled to generate 1,000 samples of actual realized price after exchange rate variance, to include having to rely upon an expensive ($5.00 per unit) price in case of outsourcing vendor failure. Table 6.1 shows these simulation parameters, which were used in a Crystal Ball model. Expected prices are generated by multiplying the quoted price by the mean exchange rate and dividing by 1 minus each probability. Thus for China 1, the probability of not failing is $(1 - 0.10)(1 - 0.15)(1 - 0.05) = 0.72675$, and this means the probability of failure is $1 - 0.72675 = 0.27325$. The cost if vendor failure is not involved is $0.82 \times 1.3 = 1.066, and the cost if failure is involved is $5.00. The expected cost is thus

$$\$0.82 \times 1.3 \times 0.72675 + \$5.00 \times 0.27325 = \$2.14.$$

Table 6.1. Simulation Distributions and Probabilities Used

	Outsourcing vendor	Quoted price	Exchange distribution	Product failure	Firm failure	Political failure	Expected price
A	China 1	0.82	Norm (1.3, 0.2)	0.10	0.15	0.05	2.14
B	China 2	0.85	Norm (1.3, 0.2)	0.09	0.15	0.05	2.14
C	China 3	0.92	Norm (1.3, 0.2)	0.07	0.13	0.05	2.08
D	Taiwan	1.36	Norm (1.03, 0.02)	0.01	0.01	0.10	1.83
E	Vietnam	0.85	Norm (1.1, 0.1)	0.15	0.25	0.05	2.54
F	Germany	3.20	Norm (0.9, 0.02)	0.01	0.02	0.01	2.96
G	Iceland	2.65	Norm (1.6, 0.3)	0.03	0.10	0.20	4.47
H	Michigan	2.40	1	0.02	0.20	0.03	3.02
I	California	3.85	1	0.01	0.25	0.03	4.17
J	Alabama	2.30	1	0.03	0.20	0.03	2.97

In this case, the first Chinese vendor had a higher probability of failure (more than 0.27 from all sources combined, compared to 0.12 for the Taiwanese vendor). This raises the mean cost, because in case of failure, the $5.00 per unit default price is used.

Monte Carlo simulation output enables identification of the distribution of prices for modeled outsourcing vendors. Table 6.2 shows the spreadsheet model, with distributions in darker shading and output cells in lighter shading. Distributions by country in column C were normal with stated mean and standard deviation. Crystal Ball has a Yes/No probability, used in columns D, E, and F, to determine failure. Survival in column G is the maximum of these three columns (vendors had to survive all three types of risk to survive). Cost was $5.00 if the vendor failed (the cost of an alternative supply), and if the vendor did not fail, the cost was the quoted price multiplied by the simulated outcome of average exchange rate inflation. Column I counted the number of cases where that vendor was the lowest realized cost. Table 6.3 shows comparative output. Simulation provides a more complete picture of the uncertainties involved.

Table 6.2. Vendor Selection Simulation Model

	A	B	C	D	E	F	G	H	I
1	Vendor	Quote	Exchange distribution	Product failure	Firm failure	Political failure	Survival	Cost	Low
2	China 1	0.82	N(1.3,.2)	Y(.1)	Y(.15)	Y(.05)	=D2*E2*F2	=IF(G2=1,B2*C2,5)	IF(H2=$H$13,1,0)
3	China 2	0.85	=C2	Y(.09)	Y(.15)	Y(.05)	=D2*E2*F2	=IF(G2=1,B2*C2,5)	IF(H3=$H$13,1,0)
4	China 3	0.92	=C2	Y(.07)	Y(.13)	Y(.05)	=D2*E2*F2	=IF(G2=1,B2*C2,5)	IF(H4=$H$13,1,0)
5	Taiwan	1.36	N(1.03,.02)	Y(.01)	Y(.01)	Y(.1)	=D2*E2*F2	=IF(G2=1,B2*C2,5)	IF(H5=$H$13,1,0)
6	Vietnam	0.85	N(1.1,.1)	Y(.15)	Y(.25)	Y(.05)	=D2*E2*F2	=IF(G2=1,B2*C2,5)	IF(H6=$H$13,1,0)
7	Germany	3.20	N(.9,.02)	Y(.01)	Y(.02)	Y(.01)	=D2*E2*F2	=IF(G2=1,B2*C2,5)	IF(H7=$H$13,1,0)
8	Iceland	2.65	N(1.6,.3)	Y(.03)	Y(.10)	Y(.2)	=D2*E2*F2	=IF(G2=1,B2*C2,5)	IF(H8=$H$13,1,0)
9	Michigan	2.40	1	Y(.02)	Y(.2)	Y(.03)	=D2*E2*F2	=IF(G2=1,B2*C2,5)	IF(H9=$H$13,1,0)
10	California	3.85	1	Y(.01)	Y(.25)	Y(.03)	=D2*E2*F2	=IF(G2=1,B2*C2,5)	IF(H10=$H$13,1,0)
11	Alabama	2.30	1	Y(.03)	Y(.2)	Y(.03)	=D2*E2*F2	=IF(G2=1,B2*C2,5)	IF(H11=$H$13,1,0)
12									
13	Low							=MIN (H2:H12)	

Column G (Survival) was calculated by the function "=D2*E2*F2" for China 1, and similarly for all other vendors. This function is 1 if the vendor survived all three risk categories modeled. The low cost realized for each run across all ten vendors was identified in cell H13.

Column H (Cost) was modeled by the function "IF(G2=1,B2*C2,5)" for China 1, yielding a cost of the quoted value inflated by the exchange rate, or a cost of $5.00 if the vendor failed that simulation run.

Column I (Low) identified the number of times each vendor was low in each of the 1,000 runs simulated.

The output of this model was provided by Crystal Ball for each vendor's cost and the proportion of times the vendor would have been the low realized cost. Table 6.3 reports the results of the simulation.

Table 6.3. Simulation Results

Vendor	Prob{Low}	Prob{Fail}	Average cost	Maximum cost
China 1	0.37	0.284	2.20	
China 2	0.10	0.272	2.19	
China 3	0.02	0.236	2.12	
Taiwan	0.02	0.119	**1.83**	
Vietnam	0.49	0.393	2.54	
Germany	0	0.046	2.98	
Iceland	0	0.304	4.46	6.56
Michigan	0	0.259	3.08	
California	0	0.297	3.85	
Alabama	0	0.256	2.99	

Figure 6.1 shows a frequency histogram for the Taiwanese source.

Note that the spike on the right is for those cases where this source failed one or more of the three risk categories, and thus was assigned an outcome of $5.00 per unit. This occurred 119 times out of 1,000 simulation runs. The cluster on the left reflects the other 881 outcomes, with a mean cost after exchange rate adjustment of slightly less than $1.50 per unit. The mean cost for these 1,000 runs came out $1.83 per unit (minimum $1.31, maximum $5.00). The Monte Carlo simulation software (here I used Crystal Ball, but the results are similar for @Risk or Frontline Solver) provides great value in entering distributions, as in Table 6.2 columns C–F, and in displaying selected outcomes, as in Figure 6.1.

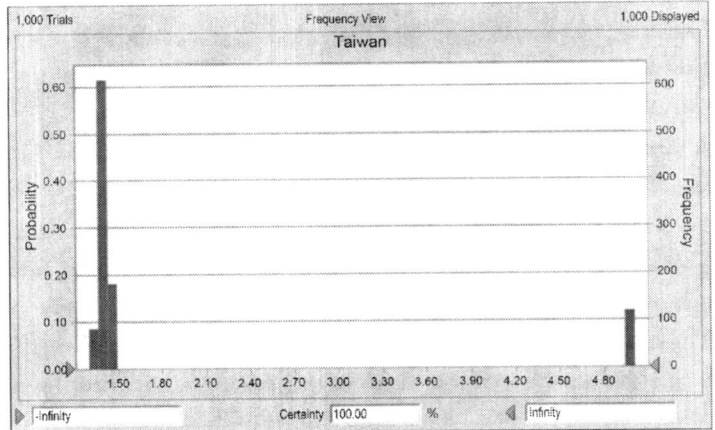

Figure 6.1. Forecast for the Taiwanese Source

Table 6.4 shows the results for the two lowest-cost alternatives, as well as the source with the least expected number of stock-outs (Germany).

Table 6.4. Source Model Statistics

Statistic	Cost, Taiwan	Cost, China 3	Cost, Germany
Mean	1.83	2.12	2.98
Median	1.41	1.29	2.88
Mode	5.00	5.00	5.00
Standard deviation	1.17	1.62	0.45
Minimum	1.31	0.67	2.69
Maximum	5.00	5.00	5.00

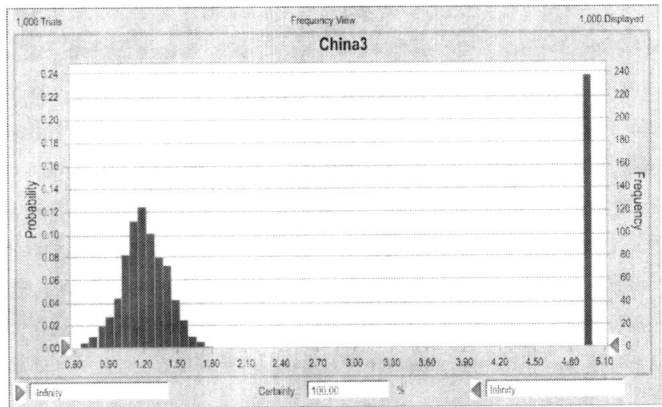

Figure 6.2. Frequency Histogram for Source China 3

Figure 6.2 displays the frequency histogram for source China 3. There is a higher probability of failure than was the case with the Taiwanese source, but also a lower cost (with greater variability).

The average costs realized are reasonably close to the calculated expected prices. Based on the probability of being the low realized cost, the Vietnamese vendor would be attractive. However, that vendor has the highest probability of failure. The lowest average cost was realized in Taiwan, which survived 88% of the simulation runs (the best probability among the ten vendors simulated). Based on average cost as well as risk avoidance, the Taiwanese vendor appears to be a good choice.

As a point of interest, the Icelandic vendor had exchange rate distribution variance high enough to have a modeled price of $6.56 in one of 1,000 simulations.

Probabilities of being the low-cost alternative are also shown. The greatest probability was for Vietnam at 0.479, with China close behind at 0.406. The expensive (but safer) alternatives of Germany and Alabama both had probabilities below 0.01 of being low, and Germany had a very high probability of survival.

The Value at Risk (VaR) Concept

Markowitz (1952) equated risk with variance, which is controlled by diversification, considering correlation across investments available, and focused on efficient portfolios not dominated with risk and return.[2] This leads to the need for some calculus of preferences, such as multiattribute utility theory.[3] Financial risk management has developed additional tools.

Value at risk is one of the most widely used models in risk management.[4] It is based on probability and statistics.[5] VaR can be characterized as a maximum expected loss, given some time horizon at a given confidence interval. Its utility is in providing a measure of risk inherent in a portfolio with multiple risk factors, such as portfolios held by large banks, which are diversified across many risk factors and product types. VaR is used to estimate the boundaries of risk for a portfolio over a given time period for an assumed probability distribution of market performance. The purpose is to diagnose risk exposure. This concept has been proposed for supply chain source selection, considering the two criteria of minimizing expected cost and minimizing the expected worst-case costs (which can be defined for specified probability levels through VaR).[6]

VaR and Vendor Selection

I will now return to the vendor selection model we used earlier in this chapter to demonstrate the concept of VaR in a supply chain context. VaR essentially looks at a worst-case scenario in a probabilistic situation at some level of risk specified by the decision maker.

Table 6.1 provides the basic input data we will use. It is the same simulation model—VaR involves a different interpretation of the output. Earlier in this chapter we focused on the average cost of each vendor, the probability of that vendor being the low bidder, and the probability of each vendor failing. VaR is a different means to identify the expected cost for each vendor at some prescribed level of probability. I will demonstrate 0.9 and 0.95 levels of probability for the cost distribution for each vendor. These provide decision makers with a gauge of relative risk involved for each.

In our data set (purely hypothetical), most of the sources had relatively high failure probabilities. Only the German source had a higher survival probability, which can be used to demonstrate the concept of VaR applied to supply chain source selection. Outcome frequency histograms for probability levels of 0.95 and 0.90 are displayed in Figures 6.3 and 6.4. Figure 6.3 shows the 0.95 level cost to be $3.04 per unit. Figure 6.4 shows the cost to be $2.98 at the 0.90 level. In both cases, Crystal Ball sorts the 1,000 outcomes, grouping them in the frequency histograms displayed in Figures 6.3 and 6.4. These figures were obtained

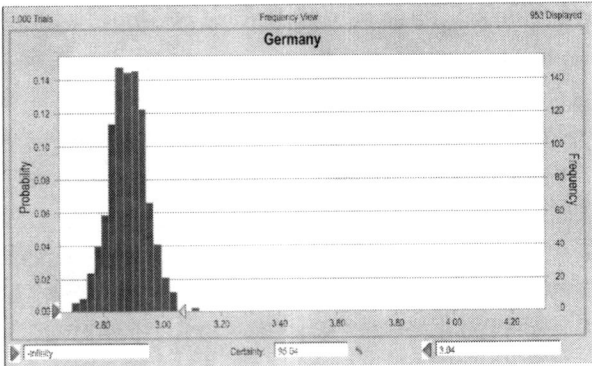

Figure 6.3. Outcomes for the German Source

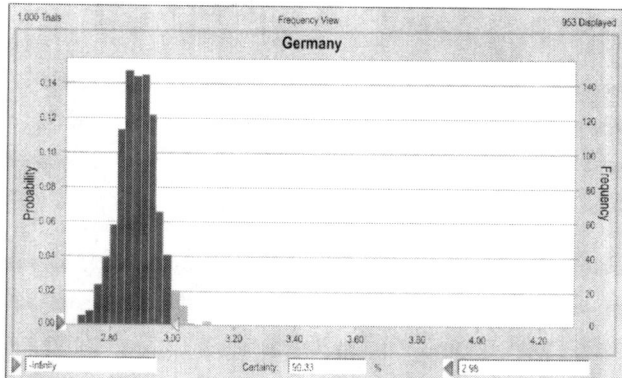

Figure 6.4. *VaR display for the German Source*

by using the grabbers on the horizontal axis, allowing the modeler to identify outcomes at chosen probability levels.

Value at risk has undesirable properties, especially for gain and loss data with nonsymmetric distributions. VaR only considers the extreme percentile of a gain/loss distribution without considering the magnitude of the loss. As a consequence, a variant of VaR, usually called conditional value at risk (CVaR), has been used. With respect to computational issues, optimization of CVaR can be very simple, which is another reason for adoption of CVaR. Rockafellar and Uryasev showed that CVaR constraints in optimization problems can be formulated as linear constraints.[7] CVaR represents a weighted average between the VaR and losses exceeding the VaR. CVaR is a risk assessment approach used to reduce the probability a portfolio will incur large losses, assuming a specified confidence level. It is possible to maximize portfolio return subject to constraints including CVaR and other downside risk measures, both absolute and relative to a benchmark (market and liability based).

Demonstration Example of Supply Chain Simulation

Eksioglu, B., Eksioglu, S., Zhang, J., and Jin, M. (2010). A simulation model to analyze the impact of outsourcing on furniture supply chain performance. *Forest Products Journal,* *60*(3), 258–265.

U.S. manufacturing has seen a massive shift to outsourcing of production to Asia (specifically to China). This is true of the furniture industry as well as many other manufacturing industries. One example is La-Z-Boy, the second largest furniture manufacturer in the United States, which shut down most of its U.S. production and moved it to China. U.S. furniture companies now focus on brand management and logistics, relying upon direct outsourcing. Upholstered furniture imports from China have grown more than 50% each year over the 10 years from 1997 through 2006. Many U.S. upholstered furniture manufacturers were located in northeastern Mississippi. The new supply chain sees production in China, shipment to Long Beach, California, rail shipment to Memphis, Tennessee, and then on to the furniture companies in northeastern Mississippi for assembly. This change has been driven by

- globalization, which has broadened competition in manufacturing;
- containerized shipping technology, which has lowered shipping costs; and
- the labor intensive nature of furniture manufacturing.

There are a number of supply chain models for furniture importing, shown in Table 6.5.

Table 6.5. Furniture Supply Chain Model Alternatives

Model	Manufacturer	Agent	Assembler	Sales
Manufacturer outsourcing	Chinese	Agent	U.S.	Wholesale/retail
Direct investment	U.S. plant in China		U.S.	Wholesale/retail
Direct sales	Chinese			Wholesale/retail
Agent outsourcing	Chinese	Agent		Wholesale/retail

A simulation model was developed to evaluate options. The model included one finished furniture product requiring one raw material. The model consisted of two alternate suppliers: Asian (cheaper unit purchasing price) and U.S. There are five customers (Portland, OR; Chicago, IL; Houston, TX; New York City, NY; and Jacksonville, FL).

Lead time for the Asian supplier ranges from 11 to 25 weeks, consisting of

- sea transportation (triangular distribution, 9–11 weeks, most likely 10 weeks);
- Long Beach, California, waiting time to unload (triangular distribution, 0–8 weeks, most likely 3 weeks);
- rail transportation from Long Beach to Memphis (triangular distribution, 12–14 days, most likely 13 days);
- Memphis waiting time to unload (triangular distribution, 0–4 weeks, most likely 1 week); and
- trucking time from Memphis to the assembly plant in Tupelo, Mississippi (constant, 1 day).

Lead time from the local supplier is assumed to be constant at 1 day, but inventory might not be available. A reorder point system is used.

Demands for each customer were assumed to be normally distributed with a mean of 10 units and a variance of 2 units. All customer orders are aggregated on one delivery day. The assembler promises a 2-week lead time if inventory is on hand.

Performance measures were inventory level, backlog, purchasing cost, percentage of orders filled on time, inventory holding cost (20% holding cost), and backorder penalties at the rate of 30% of revenue.

Simulations were run to consider various proportions of purchases from Asia, relying on local sources when the Asian source was out of stock or delivery was late or damaged. Weekly orders were assumed.

The simulation results demonstrated that outsourcing to China was not necessarily the best option due to local reduction of capacity. The industry supply chain is quite long, and U.S. forest supplies and infrastructure are diminishing. The simulation model developed enabled break-even analysis on the part of Mississippi furniture assemblers, with detailed predictions of supply chain system performance.

Conclusion

This chapter described the use of Monte Carlo simulation in a typical supply chain management selection decision. It also discussed the possible use of the VaR concept in analyzing Monte Carlo simulation output. The relevance of this decision to real supply chain management decision making was supported by the example application described.

The software used here was Crystal Ball. Excel can be used to build basic models, but it is unrealistic to consider conducting Monte Carlo simulations directly in Excel. Similar results can be obtained using other software (such as @Risk or Frontline Solver). These program provide great value in entering distributions and in displaying selected outcomes.

CHAPTER 7

Optimization Models in Supply Chain Risk Management

I have primarily discussed selection decisions in supply chain management. Another major decision type is route selection, as transportation across supply chain facilities is a major issue, as well as selection of those facilities.

Linear programming (LP) was developed as one of the original operations research tools during World War II. It provides a means to optimize a system. It is a particular type of mathematical programming that has been used to improve the efficiency of many business operations, including many supply chain operations.

Linear Programming Models in Operations Management

Linear programming is one of the most powerful analytic tools available to support operations management. LP provides the optimal, or best possible, solution to problems that can be formulated by a linear function subject to a set of linear constraints. This has proven extremely useful in many operations management applications, some of which are described in Table 7.1.

Table 7.1. Linear Programming Models Applying to Supply Chains

Type of model	Variables	Function to optimize	Typical constraints
Product mix	Number of products to produce	Maximize contribution to profit	Resource limits, such as time, labor, material; maximum or minimum quantities
Blending	Amount of materials to combine to produce one unit of product	Minimize cost	Resource limits; demand requirements
Production line scheduling	Sequence of production	Minimize cost	Resource limits; time requirements
Inventory	Number of inventory items to order by period	Minimize cost (sum of production and inventory)	On-hand minimums by time period; inventory balance equations
Transportation	Assign sources for distribution of goods to demands	Minimize cost	Capacity limits at sources; demand requirements
Assignment	Assign sources of resources to tasks	Minimize cost	Conventional sources and demand capacities equal 1

Linear programming provides a means of modeling these and other important operations management problems in order to identify more efficient methods of doing business. While LP provides a great deal of benefit, it comes with a fairly high price, in that only certain types of decision problems can be appropriately modeled with LP. This usually involves allocation of limited resources to alternative uses. The biggest drawbacks to this very powerful technique are that the decision problem must be expressed in linear functions, and since the very best possible solution is sought, minor changes in assumed coefficient values can have a drastic impact on the resulting solution.

Components

Linear programming models consist of variables, functions in terms of these variables, and limits to functions. To build an LP model of a decision problem, it is usually easiest to concentrate on the decision to be made. Those things that are within decision-maker control are usually the appropriate decision variables. Another element that often helps the modeler is to identify the objective of the decision. Usually that will be profit. The variables are those problem elements within decision-maker control that contribute to profit. If there is difficulty identifying decision variables, sometimes thinking about how profit can be measured helps that identification. The last element of the model is the set of limits to the decision. Mathematical programming is very flexible in allowing the modeler to impose limits on the decision. It is possible to limit the decision so much that there is no possible way to satisfy all the limits (infeasibility). If that happens, the crux of the decision will be what limits have to be released. The reverse case is where important limits are left out. If the resulting model solution seems impractical, the outrageous features of the solution provide clues as to missing limits.

Variables: Variables are the items that can be varied in order to improve the objective function. Typically they are things decision makers can control, such as production levels. In supply chain contexts, they can be the sources selected, or the routes assigned for transportation.

Functions: Functions are mathematical statements measuring something in terms of the variables. Profit is an example of a function. Risk is another example.

Demonstration Model

To demonstrate LP, I will present a simplified problem involving identification of a shipping schedule to deliver petroleum products from refineries to depots. The firm has refineries in Houston, Corpus Christi, and Fort Worth, Texas. It has depots in San Antonio, Bryan, and El Paso, Texas. Table 7.2 gives supply and demand volumes in thousands of gallons (on a daily basis).

Table 7.2. System Parameters

Refinery	Capacity (thousand gallons)	Depot	Requirements (thousand gallons)
Houston	150	San Antonio	200
Corpus Christi	100	Bryan	120
Fort Worth	250	El Paso	180

The costs of transporting 1,000 gallons from each refinery to each depot are given in Table 7.3.

Table 7.3. Shipping Unit Costs

Source	Depot			Supply (thousand gallons)
	(S) San Antonio	(B) Bryan	(E) El Paso	
(H) Houston	$200	$90	$50	150
(C) Corpus Christi	$60	$100	$180	100
(F) Fort Worth	$20	$150	$120	250
Demand (thousand gallons)	200	120	180	500

An LP model can be constructed to minimize transportation cost using variables for each combination of source and depot. The variables represent the quantity shipped that day over the indicated route. The coefficients in the objective function are the unit costs. Constraints are that the quantity shipped out of each refinery is less than or equal to that refinery's capacity, and that the quantity that each depot receives is at least as much supply as is needed to cover its demand:

Minimize = 200 HS + 90 HB + 50 HE + 60 CS + 100 CB + 180
   CE + 20 FS + 150 FB + 120 FE
Subject to:
   HS + HB + HE   ≤ 150
   CS + CB + CE   ≤ 100
   FS + FB + FE   ≤ 250
   HS + CS + FS   ≥ 200
   HB + CB + FB   ≥ 120

HE + CE + FE $\geq$ 180

HS, HB, HE, CS, CB, CE, FS, FB, FE $\geq$ 0

Solution

Models in Excel can be optimized with Solver, which allows you to find optimal solutions to constrained optimization problems formulated as spreadsheet models. (Check the list of available add-ins under Tools/Add-Ins. If Solver is not listed, you will have to reinstall Excel, using a custom installation, or select Add-Ins and check Solver.)

To use Solver, you should design your spreadsheet to include the following:

- A cell for each decision variable
- A cell that calculates the objective function value
- Cells for each constraint function
- A cell for each function limit

It is usually convenient to lay out your variables in rows or columns and provide descriptive labels either to the left of the columns or above the rows; this improves the readability and manageability of your models.

In Solver, decision variables are called *adjustable cells*, or *changing cells*, and the objective function cell is called the *target cell*. Solver identifies values of the changing cells that minimize or maximize the target cell value. Solver is easier to use if you define a cell for each of the constraint functions in your model (i.e., the left-hand sides of the constraints).

In the transportation model, the spreadsheet shown in Table 7.4 models the problem.

The spreadsheet contains the listing of the decision variables in cells C1 through K1. The variable cells themselves are C2 through K2. The target cell is the cost function, cell L2. The input data are found in columns C through K, rows 3 through 9. Column L contains functions. SUMPRODUCT is a useful Excel function that makes it easy to multiply one vector times another. In this case the vector of decision variable values (C2:K2) is multiplied by the coefficients in rows 3 through 9. Constraint limits are found in column N. Figure 7.1 shows the Solver window to enter this model. Table 7.5 shows the solution.

Table 7.4. Transportation LP Model

	A	B	C	D	E	F	G	H	I	J	K	L	M	N
1			HS	HB	HE	CS	CB	CE	FS	FB	FE	Function		Limit
2		quantities										=SUMPRODUCT($C$2:$K$2,C3:K3)		
3		costs	200	90	50	60	100	180	20	150	120			
4	Supplies	Houston	1	1	1							=SUMPRODUCT($C$2:$K$2,C4:K4)	≤	150
5		Corpus				1	1	1				=SUMPRODUCT($C$2:$K$2,C5:K5)	≤	100
6		Ft Worth							1	1	1	=SUMPRODUCT($C$2:$K$2,C6:K6)	≤	250
7	Demands	S Antonio	1			1			1			=SUMPRODUCT($C$2:$K$2,C7:K7)	≥	200
8		Bryan		1			1			1		=SUMPRODUCT($C$2:$K$2,C8:K8)	≥	120
9		El Paso			1			1			1	=SUMPRODUCT($C$2:$K$2,C9:K9)	≥	180

The solution is found in bold in cells C2 through K2. Total cost (which was minimized) is found in cell L2 ($28,100). In this model each supply and demand was at its limit, because in this special case, supply equaled demand.

Assumptions

A key element of LP models is the set of assumptions required. These assumptions are **linearity**, **certainty**, and **continuity**. Different functions

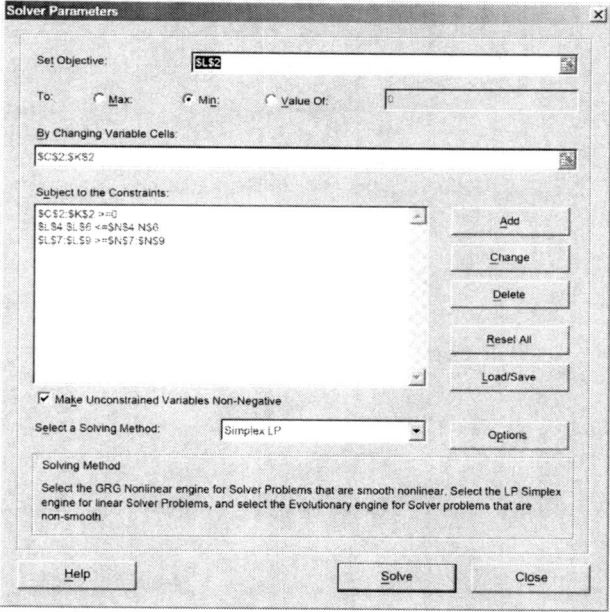

Figure 7.1. Solver Screen for the Transportation Model

could have been selected as the objective function. The optimal solution obtained is only optimal with respect to the function used as the objective.

Linearity: All functions must be linear. Often, this is no problem. In the example problem, each unit (1,000 gallons of oil) will contribute the same toward the supply or demand given in Table 7.5. Quality control is applied to make sure that this happens. The function would not truly be linear, however, if there were economies of scale available. This could happen in our models with resources such as man-hours, although if the decision produced by the model is not significantly different from current

Table 7.5. Transportation Model Solution

	A	B	C	D	E	F	G	H	I	J	K	L	M	N
			HS	HB	HE	CS	CB	CE	FS	FB	FE	Function		Limit
1														
2		quantities	0	0	150	0	100	0	200	20	30	28,100		
3		costs	200	90	50	60	100	180	20	150	120			
4	Supplies	Houston	1	1	1							150	≤	150
5		Corpus				1	1	1				100	≤	100
6		Ft Worth							1	1	1	250	≤	250
7	Demands	S Antonio	1			1			1			200	≥	200
8		Bryan		1			1			1		120	≥	120
9		El Paso			1			1			1	180	≥	180

operations, the resulting nonlinearity should not be important. In this model, labor is represented by the function CANS. One function where nonlinearity may be a problem is the objective function of profit. If the company is large enough to be able to influence the sales price with large increases in volume, diminishing returns of scale could result. That would lead to a nonlinear profit function. Here, again, this will not be a problem if the quantity in the solution is not too large relative to current production.

Certainty: The resulting LP solution will be optimal IF the coefficients used are correct. A general LP model can be expressed as

$$\text{Maximize} \sum_{j=1}^{n} c_j x_j$$

$$\text{s.t.} \sum_{j=1}^{n} a_{ij} x_j \leq b_i \text{ for } i = 1$$

$$x_j \geq 0 \text{ for } j = 1 \text{ to } n$$

There are three classes of coefficients in this model. If contribution coefficients (c_j) are estimates, or are random variables, you will get a feasible solution, but you are not guaranteed the best possible solution. If the coefficient b_i (right-hand-side values) or the technological coefficient a_{ij} are estimates with some variance, the solution may not be feasible when implemented. There is a certain degree of sensitivity analysis that can be conducted to determine how much c_j or b_i can vary before it makes any difference. There is also a limited amount of sensitivity analysis that can be accomplished if a_{ij} varies. Sensitivity analysis of a_{ij} is beyond the scope of what we want to do. The important thing to remember about certainty is that *the validity of the resulting solution depends upon the accuracy of the model coefficients*. If a coefficient varies just a bit, the resulting solution may still be useful. But a high degree of variance in coefficients invalidates the optimality of an LP solution.

Continuity: LP solutions are generally obtained with the simplex technique. That technique converts all constraints to equalities by adding slack or surplus variables. The resulting solution will be a set of variable values that simultaneously solve the entire set of equations and have the greatest (or if minimizing, the smallest) objective function value. Since the variable values are the result of simultaneously solving equations, the optimal solution may well contain fractional values. A feasible solution can usually be obtained by rounding. However, the best solution containing only integer decision variable values is not necessarily a solution with these values (in the example, it is). This can especially be a problem for variables that have to be either zero or one (for instance, do a project or don't). Sometimes the existence of noninteger solution values does not matter. If the optimal solution called for shipping 149.1 thousand gallons from Houston to El Paso, you could round to 149 thousand gallons. If it does make a difference, there are solution techniques that guarantee integer or zero-one decision variable values. (In Solver, simply add a constraint for B2:B6 to be INT [for integer]. You can also make variables be 0-1 by specifying variable cells to be BIN [for binary].

Complications

The solution of an LP model can yield a number of results. The possible results can be viewed as a tree.

The first branch is for **feasibility**. If all goes well, the model is feasible. If the constraint set includes conflicting constraints, there is no possible solution to the model. This is hopefully because one or more constraints were included that were too tight. The next branch of possible model outcomes is **boundedness**. If you have a simple model with the objective of maximizing $A + B$ subject to $A \leq 10$, there is an unlimited objective function value. B could increase infinitely. An **unbounded** solution is usually due to a missing constraint, and if the computer solution indicates an unbounded solution, that is a clue to the modeler to add some missing limit to the model. The canning example is bounded, and no problem exists. In fact, all five decision variables are individually limited.

The final branch of possible outcomes is the number of optimal solutions. We would normally expect one best (**unique optimal**) solution. LP guarantees us the best objective function value to a model. There may, however, be more than one solution yielding that optimal value (**multiple optimal solutions**). Actually, multiple optimal solutions are opportunities rather than problems, because their existence indicates there is more than one way to obtain the best possible outcome (as measured by the objective function). This will provide the decision maker with added flexibility.

Additional complications: LP solution codes take care of inserting the slack/surplus variables and obtaining the optimal solution. They work very

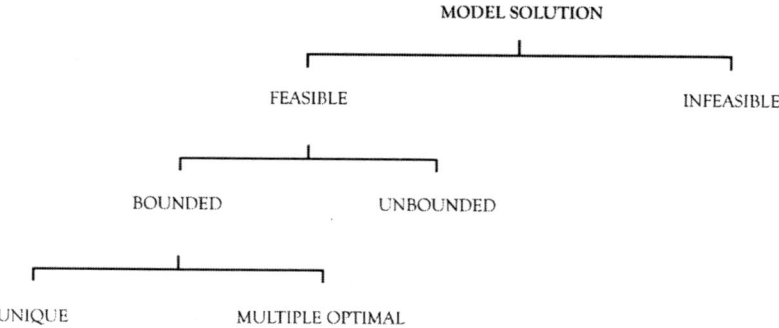

efficiently in general, although most codes have difficulty with very large models (tens of thousands of variables and thousands of constraints). Some codes have been built to deal with more than a million variables for special types of models. In general, the larger the model, the longer it takes to run on the computer. Also, because computers work in binary terms, rounding becomes a problem for large models. There is one potential source of severe problems, however. **Degeneracy** can occur when more than two constraints intersect at the same point. What happens is that the reduced costs/dual prices are not dependable, and the solution method can actually cycle. Most codes are written to minimize the risk of cycling. But care must still be taken with interpretation of reduced costs/dual prices. Potential degeneracy occurs when basic variable values of zero exist.

Reduced costs are the amount that a c_j must improve before it is attractive enough to be part of the basic solution (take on a nonzero value). The optimal decision will remain the same as long as any one c_j stays within its allowable range and *no other model coefficients change*.

Dual prices are the rate of change in the objective function per unit change in the right-hand-side coefficient. The dual price will remain constant as long as the associated b_i stays within its allowable range, and *no other model coefficients change*.

Integer Models

In the discussion about the assumption of continuity, I said that simplex was liable to give fractional decision variable values in the optimal solution. For some models, this is unacceptable. For instance, you cannot physically have 0.48 of a building, or buy 0.85 automobiles.

There is absolutely no problem modeling those cases where integer or zero-one restrictions on the variables are required. Simply specify variables by the appropriate class and add these specifications to the model. There *is* a problem *solving* these classes of models.

Excel's Solver takes care of all of this logic. All you have to do to obtain an integer solution is constrain the selected variables to be INT (an integer), as demonstrated below.

Zero-One Programming

Zero-one variables are very useful in a number of operations management contexts, such as plant scheduling (where machine setups are required between production runs for different products) and inventory models (where orders are placed with a cost independent of order quantity).

I will demonstrate this concept with another simple LP model, in this case dealing with inventory management. A supply chain has a fairly stable demand, with reasonably reliable forecasts of sales demands. Prices are increasing. Stock can be purchased early at cheaper purchase prices, but this would include carrying costs, which are 10% of the purchase price at the beginning period where the inventory is held. Purchase prices are $10 per unit in periods 1 and 2, and $11 per unit in periods 3 and 4. Demands are 800 units in period 1, 900 units in period 2, 1,000 units in period 3, and 1,200 units in period 4. There is a fixed cost per order of $100.

The LP model has variables for demand (D1, D2, D3, and D4) that are set to their forecast values, quantities purchased per period (P1, P2, P3, and P4), quantities carried forward as inventory (I12, I23, and I34), and fixed ordering costs (F1, F2, F3, and F4). The fixed ordering costs are zero-one variables. The profit function is $15 for each item sold (D1–D4) minus the costs of purchase, inventory, and ordering:

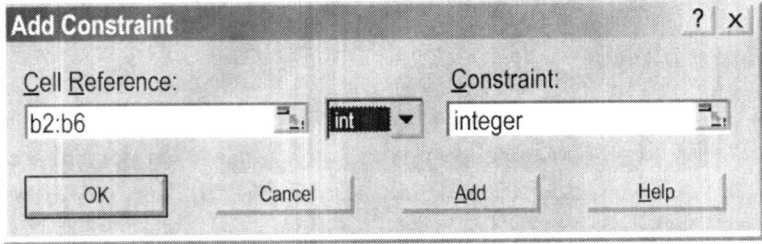

Maximum – 100 F1 – 100 F2 – 100 F3 – 100 F4 + 15 D1 + 15
   D2 + 15 D3 + 15 D4 – 10 P1 – 10 P2 – 11 P3 – 11 P4 – 1
   I12 – 1 I23 – 1.1 I34

Subject to

1. D1 – P1 + I12 = 0
2. D2 – P2 – I12 + I23   = 0
3. D3 – P3 – I23 + I34   = 0
4. D4 – P4 – I34 = 0
5. D1 = 800
6. D2 = 900
7. D3 = 1,000
8. D4 = 1,200
9. P1 – 9,999 F1 ≤ 0
10. 1   P2   – 9,999 F2   ≤ 0
11. 1   P3   – 9,999 F3   ≤ 0
12. 1   P4   – 9,999 F4   ≤ 0
13. 1   D1, D2, D3, D4, P1, P2, P3, P4, I12, I23, I34 ≥ 0
14. 1   F1, F2, F3, F4 = (0 or1)

The solution is shown in Table 7.6.

This solution yields a total profit of $12,780.

Hopefully the following case demonstrates some of the potential of optimization models for better organizational management.

Supply Chain Demonstration Model

Metals production, such as steel or aluminum, involves global supply chains with many competitive industries. The World Bank has generated complex mathematical programming models for the aluminum[1] and petroleum industries to help them evaluate investment proposals in developing countries. The aluminum industry consists of four levels of facilities:

1. mines—located worldwide, where bauxite is obtainable at highly variable costs;
2. refineries—facilities requiring heavy investment to convert bauxite to aluminum oxide;

Table 7.6. Inventory Model Solution

Period	Demands	Purchases	End inventories	Orders
1	800	3,900	3,100	1
2	900	0	2,200	0
3	1,000	0	1,200	0
4	1,200	0	0	0
Profit	+58,500	−39,000	−6,620	−100

3. smelters—facilities using massive quantities of electricity to convert aluminum oxide into aluminum; and

4. demands—wholesale distributors of aluminum to many industries (e.g., construction, automotive).

These four facility levels are all connected by transportation routes. In principle, the output of any mine, refinery, or smelter can be shipped up the supply chain to the next level of facility. The costs of transportation vary significantly, of course. An LP model can be used to include capacity limitations for each facility, shrinkage rates specific to each combination of facilities (10 tons of bauxite might yield 4 tons of aluminum oxide, which in turn might yield 2 tons of aluminum).

We assume a supply chain with three mines, located in Arkansas, Jamaica, and Guyana; two refineries, located in Jamaica and Texas; two smelters, located near Seattle and in Tennessee; and three demand wholesalers, in New York, Chicago, and Los Angeles. Shipping is physically possible between all three, but political restrictions limit Jamaican ore to use in the Jamaica refinery. The LP model is the following:

Minimize	Cost
Subject to	
Risk function	≤ specified limit
Capacities	≤ limits for each mine, refinery, and smelter
Shipped	= received for each source–destination combination
Output*shrink	= input at the next stage for each receiving facility
Each variable	≥ 0

Table 7.7. Model Parameters

Variable	Cost ($)	Risk	Capacity (T)	Shrink
Mine Arkansas	2	0.1	5,000	0.4
Mine Jamaica	1	0.8	5,000	0.4
Mine Guyana	1.1	1	10,000	0.4
Arkansas to Texas	0.5			
Jamaica to Jamaica	0.2			
Guyana to Jamaica	0.7			
Guyana to Texas	0.3			
Refinery Jamaica	12	0.8	2,000	0.5
Refinery Texas	15	0.1	4,000	0.5
Jamaica to Seattle	1.8			
Jamaica to Tennessee	1.2			
Texas to Seattle	1.5			
Texas to Tennessee	1.8			
Smelter Seattle	50	0.1	1,000	
Smelter Tennessee	60	0.1	2,000	
Seattle to New York	2.2			
Seattle to Chicago	1.5			
Seattle to Los Angeles	0.7			
Tennessee to New York	1.3			
Tennessee to Chicago	0.9			
Tennessee to Los Angeles	1.8			

The solution minimizing cost is shown in Table 7.8.

Table 7.8. Basic Cost Minimization Solution

	Mine Arkansas	Mine Jamaica	Mine Guyana	Refinery Jamaica	Refinery Texas	Smelter Seattle	Smelter Tennessee
Refinery Jamaica		5,000					
Refinery Texas			7,500				
Smelter Seattle				2,000			
Smelter Tennessee					3,000		
New York							1,000
Chicago						300	500
Los Angeles						700	

The total cost for this solution is $234,190, with a risk measure of 13,650.

Risk control can be included by lowering the risk function. All that modeling requires is to place a constraint limit on the risk function. Table 7.9 shows the results of five models constrained to lower risk.

Table 7.9. Aluminum Supply Chain Solutions

	Minimum cost	Risk < 13,000	Risk < 12,000	Risk < 11,000	Risk < 10,000	Risk < 9,000
Cost ($)	234,190	234,984	236,207	237,429	238,651	242,090
Risk	13,650	13,000	12,000	11,000	10,000	9,000
Arkansas–Texas		722.2	1,833	2,944	4,056	5,000
Jamaica–Jamaica	5,000	5,000	5,000	5,000	5,000	3,125
Guyana–Texas	7,500	6,778	5,667	4,556	3,444	4,375
Guyana–Jamaica						
Jamaica–Seattle	2,000	2,000	2,000	2,000	2,000	1,250
Jamaica–Tennessee						
Texas–Seattle						750
Texas–Tennessee	3,000	3,000	3,000	3,000	3,000	3,000
Seattle–New York						
Seattle–Chicago	300	300	300	300	300	300
Seattle–Los Angeles	700	700	700	700	700	700
Tennessee–New York	1,000	1,000	1,000	1,000	1,000	1,000
Tennessee–Chicago	500	500	500	500	500	500
Tennessee–Los Angeles						

The low-cost solution involves economically attractive production in Guyana and Jamaica. Jamaica has a risk rating much lower than Guyana. As the risk function is constrained to be lower, it can be seen that

Arkansas production is increased until, in the right-hand column, it is at its capacity limit. Jamaican mining production is level until the last solution, when the riskier Guyana production increases. This is because at the refining stage, Texas has a lower risk factor than Jamaica, which compensates for the added mining risk in Guyana relative to Jamaica.

Note that the smelter-to-demand volumes are very stable. That is because the risk function is at a minimum for U.S. facilities and all of the smelters included in this model are in the United States.

Example Supply Chain Optimization Model

> Dauzère-Pérès, S., Nordli, A., Olstad, A., Haugen, K., Koester, U., Myrstad, P. O., ... Reistad, A. (2007). Omya Hustadmarmor optimizes its supply chain for delivering calcium carbonate slurry to European paper manufacturers. *Interfaces, 37*(1), 39–51.

Omya Hustadmarmor is a Norwegian company providing calcium carbonate slurry to paper manufacturers in Europe.[2] Calcium carbonate is used as a filler and coating pigment, especially in high-quality paper. A major issue in their operations is minimization of transportation costs. A decision support system (DSS) was built for maritime inventory routing. The key component of the DSS was an optimization model to make better, faster decisions.

The primary material in this slurry production is marble stone, from quarries in Norway. Omya Hustadmarmor converts this marble stone into slurry through wet grinding, adding water and chemicals. The firm ships 15 to 16 different variants of slurry to paper mills, storing them en route in 10 first-tier tank farms spread throughout northern Europe. Second-tier tank farms are located near major customers. Shipping requires chemical tank vessels, as well as barge, rail, or truck transport from tank farms to paper mills. Omya Hustadmarmor uses its own shipping as well as that of a Norwegian shipping firm. These ships service spot markets, such as Russian methanol, when they are not required to ship slurry. Shipping is a major part of total product costs.

The shipping decision is to decide which vessel should depart on which day to cover required material movements, as well as what product mix to place on each ship. Planners need to ensure that tank farm inventories don't get too low, thus threatening paper mill production. Omya Hustadmarmor has never had a stock-out failure, in part because they maintain relatively high safety stocks. This is aided by the relatively low inventory holding cost of slurry. However, this requires a lot of tank farm storage space.

Slurry is quite dense, meaning that ships have extra volume capacity when they ship slurry. This complicates matters, as ships should be at least 60% full to avoid dangerous sloshing of cargo in stormy weather. A major risk factor is the uncertainty of both demand and supply. This requires frequent plan revisions. On the supply side, ships may be delayed by bad weather or diverted by spot market activity. Demands are uncertain primarily because of the diversity of paper products supported, and the resultant change in slurry product mix.

About 2000, Omya Hustadmarmor made a strategic decision to limit capacity investments, relying more on efficient scheduling of shipping. An integer-programming mathematical model was developed with a nonlinear objective function to minimize the sum of transportation and inventory costs over their planning horizon of 84 days, including product demands and nonlinear transportation costs. Model variables were 0-1 representations of vessels assigned to leave a particular factory on a particular day. The model constrained storage capacities and included minimum quantities by product per vessel, as well as vessel availability and daily loading capacity. A genetic local search algorithm was implemented to deal with the model's nonlinearity. The optimization model was encoded in C++ with user interfaces of Excel sheets with visual basic macros to automatically format and update spreadsheets.

The system increased predictability and flexibility throughout the supply chain and was credited with savings of about $7 million per year, expected to grow with company expansion. The DSS also enabled the firm to avoid additional investment in capacity and reduced overall oil consumption by more than 10%. The system also enabled rapid replanning to cope with ship delays, machine breakdowns, and other disruptions.

Mixed-integer Optimization of Transportation Plans[3]

Storage and distribution of medical supplies is critical to disaster management. Onur Mete and Zabinsky provided a mathematical formulation in the form of an optimization model to select a subset of warehouses for the storage of medical supplies for postdisaster use that considers probabilistic inputs (Table 7.10).

The information flow in disaster management includes four entities and a number of data elements. The entities include a planning and responding team of humans, supported by three mathematical programming models.

The preparedness phase took four inputs (disaster scenarios, transportation conditions, demand estimates, and warehouse parameters) and processed this data through a stochastic programming model that yielded recommended inventory levels by supply item as well as recommended warehouse facilities. This information was passed on to the human planning and responding team, which refined the stochastic programming model in terms of hospital priorities. Output from the revised stochastic programming model was fed into a mixed integer programming model to yield transportation plans. The human team then provided further priorities to the response phase mixed integer programming model, which took supply data, demand data, and transportation conditions to generate transportation plans.

Table 7.10. Canadian Forces Medical Supply System

Inputs	Processes	Outputs
Disaster scenarios Transportation conditions Demand estimates Warehouse parameters	Stochastic programming model	Recommended warehouses → planning & responding Inventory levels Hospital priorities
Transportation conditions Stochastic prog output	Mixed Integer Model	Transportation plans → planning & responding
Stochastic prog output Mixed integer output	Planning & responding team	Hospital priorities → mixed integer model
Supply data Demand data Transportation conditions	Mixed integer model	Transportation plans → planning & responding team

This system was applied to planning inventory levels of medical supplies at warehouses with predetermined transportation plans for the Seattle area. Seattle is on two earthquake fault systems (the Seattle fault and the Cascadia fault). The statistical analysis of historical data enables the calculation of expected damage to homes, warehouses, and buildings, transportation systems, and utilities. Population densities around hospitals were available. Analysis divided three daily periods: working hours, rush hours, and nonworking hours. Six disaster scenarios were generated, with 48 working hours, 30 rush hours, and 90 nonworking hours per week. Relative probabilities for each fault for each period were identified. Estimated demand in terms of patients were generated for each of 10 hospitals. Five warehouses were modeled, each having existing capacities and operating cost rates. Transportation times between warehouses and hospitals were all available. Vehicle capacities were considered by warehouse. Ninety routes were generated connecting warehouses with a series of hospitals.

The stochastic programming model identified a plan to use three of the five warehouses for storage of medical supplies. The mixed integer programming model took this solution as input and generated routes for vehicle assignments. This output was used by the planning team to analyze bottlenecks and adjust vehicle assignments by warehouse.

Conclusion

Channel or route selection is one of the most important and longest-studied decisions in supply chain operations. The original operations research work in World War II included convoy scheduling and routing decisions. The importance of these decisions continues today, with added complexity due to the many options available in global supply chain operations. Overall supply chain management, including assignment of production quotas, is also possible, as demonstrated by the very scaled-down aluminum example.

Linear programming is one of the most powerful analytic tools available for decision support systems. LP provides a means to generate solutions that are optimal for the given objective function. Not only is the best possible decision (relative to the objective function) promised, but economic interpretation of the limits to the decision are available.[4] However, the conclusions to be drawn from LP are highly sensitive to the accuracy of the model. Errors in data or changes in demands, costs, or resource usage can make major differences. This is because, by definition, LP seeks the very best possible solution, squeezing the last bit of objective function value from the constraint set. Thus, while LP is extremely attractive, it is extremely dangerous, and the assumptions required are more difficult to satisfy.

CHAPTER 8

Balanced Scorecard in Supply Chain Management

Balanced scorecards are one of a number of quantitative tools available to support risk planning.[1] This approach was proposed initially for general strategic management support, focusing on four perspectives:

1. customer—how customers see the organization;
2. financial—how shareholders see the organization;
3. internal business—what the organization must excel at; and
4. innovation and learning—where can the organization continue to improve and create value?

This framework of measures was proposed as a means to link intangible assets to value creation for shareholders. Scorecards provide a focus on strategic objectives (goals) and measures, and have been applied in many businesses and governmental organizations with reported success. Table 8.1 shows the goals and measures proposed in the Kaplan and Norton (1992) article, specifically applied to a hypothetical technology engineering firm.

Based on Table 8.1, the **financial perspective** can be used to monitor the performance of selected outsourcing vendors in terms of their financial and market share measures. This would require agreements that would allow the core supply chain vendor to have access to outsourcing vendor internal data, which may be problematic. However, large organizations such as Walmart[2] and Dell[3] have obtained such intrusive access. This is an issue that needs to be addressed. It seems preferable to leave internal operations to the outsourced vendor, and if they fail, to return to the outsourcing market and obtain a replacement.

Table 8.1. Sample Balanced Scorecard

Perspective	Goals	Measures
Customer	• New products • Responsive supply • Preferred supplier • Customer partnership	• Percentage of sales from new products • Percentage of sales from proprietary products • On-time delivery by customer • Share of key accounts' purchases • Ranking by key accounts • Number of cooperative engineering efforts
Financial	• Survival • Success • Prospering	• Cash flow • Quarterly sales growth and operating income by division • Increase in market share and return on equity
Internal business	• Technology capability • Manufacturing excellence • Design • New products	• Comparison with competition • Cycle time • Unit cost • Yield • Efficiency • Actual versus planned
Innovation and learning	• Technology leadership • Manufacturing learning • Product focus • Time to market	• Time to develop next generation • Process time to maturity • Percentage of products equaling 80% of sales • New product introduction versus competition

With respect to **customer perspective**, the performance of the outsourcing vendor can be monitored in terms of service delivery. Cooperative efforts can be pursued to expand lines, as well as to identify methods improvement. The core supply chain organization can also monitor the share of their volume given to each outsourced vendor. It would be prudent to keep the proportion of volume to each vendor within prescribed maximum limits to avoid the risk of the outsourcing vendor failing. Again, in that contingency, you can return to the market to find replacement sources.

Measurement of **internal business operations** of the outsourcing organization also involves potential intrusion. The same issue exists as with the financial perspective. Sometimes close contractual relationships can be developed to allow the core supply chain organization to measure detailed technological and manufacturing aspects of the outsourcing vendor. In general, it seems preferable to leave these matters to the vendor.

The last balanced scorecard perspective is **innovation and learning**. These factors seem reasonable to measure from the core supply chain organization's perspective. Cooperative efforts to work with outsourcing vendors will benefit all members of the extended supply chain.

The basic idea is that the organization can track these measures over time to get a detailed picture over all four perspectives of organizational performance. The concept has been reported in many contexts and is now a standard approach to deal with measuring strategic importance. Various forms of scorecards (e.g., company-configured scorecards or strategic scorecards) have been suggested to build into the business decision support system or expert system in order to monitor the performance of the enterprise in strategic decision analysis.[4]

While risks need to be managed, taking risks is fundamental to doing business. Profit, by necessity, requires accepting some risk. Scorecards have been successfully associated with risk management at Mobil, Chrysler, the U.S. Army, and numerous other organizations.[5]

Enterprise risk can include a variety of factors with potential impact on an organization's activities, processes, and resources. External factors can result from economic change, financial market developments, and dangers arising in political, legal, technological, and demographic environments. Most of these are beyond the control of a given organization, although organizations can prepare and protect themselves in time-honored ways. Internal risks include human error, fraud, systems failure, and disrupted production, among others. Often, systems are assumed to be in place to detect and control risk, but inaccurate numbers are generated for various reasons.[6]

ERM and Balanced Scorecards

While many firms focus on Sarbanes–Oxley compliance, there is a need to consider strategic, market, and reputation risks as well. Balanced scorecards explicitly link risk management to strategic performance. An example balanced scorecard for supply chain management is outlined in Table 8.2.

Table 8.2. Supply Chain Management Balanced Scorecard

Measure	Goals	Measures
Learning and growth for employees To achieve our vision, how will we sustain our ability to change and improve?	• Increase employee ownership over process • Improve information flows across supply chain stages • Increase employee identification of potential supply chain disruptions **Risk-related goals:** • Increase employee awareness of supply chain risks • Increase supplier accountability for disruptions • Increase employee awareness of integration of supply chain and other enterprise risks	• Employee survey scores • Changes in information reports and frequencies across supply chain partners • Comparison of actual disruptions with reports about drivers of potential disruptions • Number of employees attending risk management training • Supplier contract provisions addressing risk management accountability and penalties • Number of departments participating in supply chain risk identification and assessment workshops
Internal business processes To satisfy our stakeholders and customers, where must we excel in our business processes?	• Reduce waste generated across the supply chain • Shorten time from start to finish • Achieve unit cost reductions **Risk-related goals:** • Reduce probability and impact of threats to supply chain processes • Identify specific tolerances for key supply chain processes • Reduce the number of exchanges of supply chain risks to other enterprise processes	• Pounds of scrap • Time from raw material purchase to product/service delivery to customer • Unit costs per product/service delivered, percentage of target costs achieved • Number of employees attending risk management training • Number of process variances exceeding specified acceptable risk tolerances • Extent of risks realized in other functions from supply chain process risk drivers

Measure	Goals	Measures
Customer satisfaction To achieve our vision, how should we appear to our customers?	• Improve product/service quality • Improve timeliness of product/service delivery • Improve customer perception of value **Risk-related goals:** • Reduce customer defections • Monitor threats to product/service reputation • Increase customer feedback	• Number of customer contact points • Time from customer order to delivery • Customer scores of value • Number of customers retained • Extent of negative coverage in business press of quality • Number of completed customer surveys about delivery comparisons to other providers
Financial performance To succeed financially, how should we appear to our stakeholders?	• Higher profit margins • Improved cash flows • Revenue growth **Risk-related goals:** • Reduce threats from price competition • Reduce cost overruns • Reduce costs outside the supply chain from supply chain processes	• Profit margin by supply chain partner • Net cash generated over supply chain • Increase in number of customers and sales per customer; percentage of annual return on supply chain assets • Number of customer defections due to price • Surcharges paid, holding costs incurred, overtime charges applied • Warranty claims incurred, legal costs paid, sales returns processed

Source: Developed from Beasley, Chen, Nunez, and Wright (2006).[7]

Other examples of balanced scorecard use have been presented as well, as tools providing measurements on a broader, strategic perspective. Balanced scorecards have been applied to internal auditing in accounting[8] and to mental health governance.[9] Janssen, Lienin, Gassmann, and Wokaun (2006)[10] applied a system dynamics model to the marketing of natural gas vehicles, considering the perspective of 16 stakeholders ranging from automobile manufacturers and customers to the natural gas industry and government. Policy options were compared using balanced scorecards with the following strategic categories of analysis:

- natural gas vehicle subsidies;
- fueling station subsidies;
- compressed natural gas tax reductions; and
- natural gas vehicle advertising effectiveness.

Balanced scorecards provided a systematic focus on strategic issues, allowing the analysts to examine the nonlinear responses of policy options as modeled with system dynamics. Five indicators were proposed to measure the progress of market penetration:

- ratio of natural gas vehicles per compressed natural gas fueling stations;
- type coverages (how many different natural gas vehicle types were available);
- natural gas vehicle investment payback time;
- sales per type; and
- subsidies par automobile.

Balanced Scorecards Applied to Subcontractors

The first example I will review applies a balanced scorecard to evaluation of construction subcontractors,[11] a particular type of local supply chain. The four perspectives of balanced scorecards were considered in light of the construction subcontracting context, leading to generation of criteria and measures as shown in Table 8.3.

Table 8.3. Construction Subcontracting Criteria and Measures

Perspective	Objectives	Measures	Units
Financial	Profitability	Profit/revenue	Percent
	Growth	Current revenue/ previous year	Percent
	Activity	Current revenue/ current capital	Percent
	Stability	3-year average of total sales	Dollars (millions)
	Stability	Credit rating	Certified rating

Perspective	Objectives	Measures	Units
Internal (process)	Construction management	Design review/engineering capability	Likert scale
		Project management execution	Likert scale
	Quality management	Rework rate	Percent
		Quality management execution	Likert scale
	Environmental management	Environmental friendly rate	Percent
		Environmental management execution	Likert scale
	Safety management	Accidents in 3 years	Count
		Safety management execution	Likert scale
Customer (service)	Cost	Cost variance	Percent
	Schedule	Schedule variance	Percent
	Quality	Defects per project	Percent
		Customer satisfaction rate	Percent
	Competitiveness	Contracts in 3 years	Count
		Information and work support	Count
Innovation and learning (improvement)	Technical ability	Patents	Count
		Number of technicians	Count
	Subcontractor competitiveness	Collaboration	Likert scale
		Awards minus warnings	Count
	Organization culture	Cooperation and communication	Likert scale
		Site management	Likert scale

Source: Based on Eom, Yun, and Paek (2008).

This input was then used to develop a multicriteria analysis using an analytic hierarchy process. This could be accomplished in the same manner with SMART (which was covered in chapter 4). Multicriteria analysis is usually applied for purposes of making a decision, but here the intent is to support the balanced scorecard purpose of monitoring performance, using SMART to provide a single value. It still would be wise to monitor performance within each perspective. Eom, Yun, and Paek (2008) cited the critical nature of contractor–subcontractor relationships in construction. The balanced scorecard framework, enhanced with the multicriteria analysis, was used to provide a standard, clearly understandable method for evaluating subcontractors, thus enhancing the management of this type of supply chain.

Balanced Scorecard Example[12]

Ports play an obvious role in shipping supply chains. Management of ports can be critical in smoothing operations that affect firms as well as governments (who rely on customs duties as well as having the need to foster economic activity).

Duran and Cordova analyze decisions made by a Port Authority, autonomous from the State that owns facilities and infrastructure. It interacts between shippers and cargo movers as well as coordinates with State regulation. Cargo movers include companies with equipment and facilities to accomplish the physical activity involved with imports and exports. A great deal of knowledge management is required to make trade activity work. Table 8.4 displays processes involved in trade logistics.

Table 8.4. Processes by Import/Export

Preimport processes	Preexport processes	Terminal import processes	Terminal export processes
Receiving	Receiving	Cargo receipt	Cargo receipt
Safety	Safety	Delivery	Exchange
Documentation	Documentation	Exchange	Receiving stacking
Dispatch	Physical inspection	Control departure notice	Receipt consolidation
	Document inspection		Receipt stocking
	Dispatch preparation		Receipt storage
	Coordination		Transport dispatch
	Dispatch		Shipping
	Unloading coordination		Stowing

These processes all involve knowledge and data that needs to be managed. Duran and Cordova outlined objectives in the balanced scorecard context for management of the port community, shown in Table 8.5.

Table 8.5. Port Community Balanced Scorecard

Perspectives	Strategic productivity objectives	Strategic growth objectives
Financial	Earnings before interest, taxes, depreciation, and amortization (EBITDA)	Return on assets (ROA)
Client	Traffic movement	Gross value added (GVA)
Internal Process	Mean terminal productivity	Average rate of gate attention
Learning & Growth	Result of exploitation	Rate of approved electronic documents

EBITDA measures profitability, important to monitor by company in the port community. ROA measures profitability of assets. These financial indicators provide a means to identify potential system failures. Traffic growth is a strategic objective of port clients. GVA measures the difference between a company's inputs and outputs, and indicates profit or loss before tax. Mean terminal productivity is an index measuring cargo transferred in by volume. The average rate of gate attention monitors delays for trucks bringing and/or receiving cargo. The result of exploitation measures the annual operations of a business. The rate of approved electronic documents focuses on the number of documents approved in one day, the ratio of approved documents to total documents. The influence was seen as working up Table 8.5. The result of exploitation was seen as influencing mean terminal productivity and average rate of gate attention, while a higher rate of approved electronic documents was seen as a factor in improving the average rate of gate attention. Mean terminal productivity was seen as a factor in positively affecting traffic movement as well as GVA. The average rate of gate attention was seen as a positive factor in improving GVA. GVA impact was seen as playing a role in improving EBITDA, while improved traffic movement was seen as positively impacting ROA.

The port community consists of interacting members cooperating in maintaining the flow of trade, which benefits stakeholders in different ways. The balanced scorecard framework helps identify indicators that monitor port efficiency.

Petroleum Supply Chain Balanced Scorecard

Varma, S., & Deshmukh, S. G. (2009). Evaluating petroleum supply chain performance: Overcoming shortcomings of balanced scorecard. *Global Journal of Flexible Systems Management, 10*(4), 11–22.

The balanced scorecard was applied to a petroleum supply chain with the purpose of assessing overall performance. Traditionally the focus has been on financial measures, but firm survival does not depend on profitability alone. Financial measures do not necessarily relate to strategic performance, nor are they directly related to operational effectiveness. The balanced scorecard framework was adjusted in the context of a petroleum supply chain.[13]

Petroleum supply chains have features calling for specific focus. Fluctuations in crude oil prices are widely known, calling for agility on the part of petroleum supply chain participants. It is important that crude oil quality be maintained. Traditional balanced scorecards have weaknesses in three areas:

1. The relative weight of different metrics are not considered.
2. Benchmarking with competitors is not directly available.
3. Dissimilar metrics across perspectives or measures are difficult to combine.

The cited analysis derived strategic objectives specific to petroleum supply chains and applied a multicriteria analysis to develop weights across measures. It was contended that this model could then allow comparison of organizations across the supply chain. Strategic objectives in a petroleum supply chain were generated for each of the four perspectives, along with measures as shown in Table 8.6.

Table 8.6. Petroleum Supply Chain Objectives and Measures

Perspective	Objectives	Measures	Units
Financial	Raw material price	Variation/year	Standard deviation
	Supply chain length	Days—dispatch to delivery	Days
	Physical risk	Cost to manage risk	Insurance premiums
	Market share	Annual change in market share	Percent
Internal	Steady supply	Raw material flow variation	Ratio—supply range to average
	Transportation	Cost	Dollars per metric ton
	Inventory	Value	Inventory turns
	Enterprise optimization	Efficient resource use	Likert scale
	Volume flexibility	Minimum delivered	Liters or kilograms
Customer	Product purity	Customer complaints	Percent complaining
	Steady supply	Time product available	Days per year
Innovation and learning	Use of information technology	Employees using information technology	Percent
	Postponement	Time postponed	Days

Source: Based on Varma & Deshmukh (2009).

The method used to generate weights was parallel to the SMART methodology presented in chapter 4. Others have proposed similar multicriteria analysis to enhance balanced scorecards in supply chains.[14] This modification of the balanced scorecard was intended to provide a more complete implementation, allowing a single value for overall organizational performance as in the construction example. Here the purpose also specifically included benchmarking organizational performance with competitor organizations within each perspective.

Demonstration Example

We can use the vendor selection model used in chapter 6 to demonstrate Monte Carlo simulation and apply that to demonstrate balanced scorecard analysis supported by SMART. That scenario considered a quoted price with an exchange rate distribution, a probability for product failure, a probability for firm failure, and a probability for political failure. The purpose in chapter 6 was selection. The purpose of balanced scorecards is different—it is to monitor performance (after vendor relationships are established). We thus need to change the context and assume that the 10 vendors are alternate providers of input to the supply chain system monitored on each perspective of the balanced supply chain.

The simulation viewed everything from a financial perspective. We can use the balanced scorecard framework to treat expected costs at a normalized risk level to reflect 90% confidence prices for the financial perspective, the probability of firm failure times and probability of political failure to reflect the internal perspective, the probability of product failure to reflect the customer perspective, and provide additional input to reflect firm innovation and learning input. Table 8.7 provides these data, which can be viewed here as assessments of how well each vendor performs in each category on a 0–1 scale (with 0 being the worst possible performance and 1 being the best):

Table 8.7. Balanced Scorecard Perspectives of Global Outsourcing

ID	Vendor	Financial	Internal	Customer	Innovation
A	China 1	0.90	0.70	0.50	0.40
B	China 2	0.90	0.70	0.55	0.45
C	China 3	0.93	0.80	0.65	0.60
D	Taiwan	1.00	1.00	1.00	0.80
E	Vietnam	0.80	0.30	0.30	0.30
F	Germany	0.65	0.95	1.00	1.00
G	Iceland	0.10	0.85	0.90	0.70
H	Michigan	0.64	0.60	0.95	0.85
I	California	0.40	0.50	1.00	1.00
J	Alabama	0.60	0.60	0.90	0.80

The balanced scorecard purpose of benchmarking can be supported with this analysis. Financially the risks in Iceland give this source major disadvantages. The source in Vietnam has internal issues, there are problems with product quality, and there is insufficient innovation and learning. The third Chinese source looks to be performing better on all four perspectives than the other two, but product quality and innovation and learning are areas with opportunities for improvement. The German vendor looks very good, except it is expensive. The Taiwanese source also looks very strong, although there is room for improvement in terms of innovation and learning.

Swing weighting can be applied, as was demonstrated in chapter 4 (and as was applied in the examples just presented in this chapter), to obtain weights for the four criteria (the balanced scorecard perspectives) as follows:

Rank	Assigned	Weight
1—Customer	100	0.333
2—Financial	90	0.300
3—Innovation	70	0.233
4—Internal	40	0.134
Total		1.000

The value function can be obtained as shown in Table 8.8.

Table 8.8. Balanced Scorecard Values

Perspective	Financial	Internal	Customer	Innovation	Value
Weight	0.300	0.134	0.333	0.233	
China 1	0.90	0.70	0.50	0.40	0.623
China 2	0.90	0.70	0.55	0.45	0.652
China 3	0.93	0.80	0.65	0.60	0.742
Taiwan	1.00	1.00	1.00	0.80	**0.953**
Vietnam	0.80	0.30	0.30	0.30	0.450
Germany	0.65	0.95	1.00	1.00	**0.888**
Iceland	0.10	0.85	0.90	0.70	0.607
Michigan	0.64	0.60	0.95	0.85	0.787
California	0.40	0.50	1.00	1.00	0.753
Alabama	0.60	0.60	0.90	0.80	0.747

Table 8.6 can be used to monitor performance by comparing scores of alternate sources by perspective. The overall value score can be used to rank vendor performance (possibly useful in annual contract renegotiations). In this case the numbers indicate that the Taiwanese vendor

would have the greatest value, followed some distance behind by the German vendor. The source in Vietnam scored very low, with price advantages not compensating for deficiencies in the other perspectives. The Icelandic source might be attractive except for major problems with the financial perspective.

This is a very simple example of value analysis. The example cases demonstrated had more complex hierarchies of criteria, which involves expansion of the four perspectives of financial, internal, customer, and innovation and learning with multiple measures included within each.

Conclusion

Balanced scorecard analysis provides a means to measure multiple strategic perspectives. The basic principle is to select four diverse areas of strategic importance, and within each, to identify concrete measures that managers can use to determine how their organization performs on multiple scales. This allows consideration of multiple perspectives or stakeholders as well as supply chain risk analysis.

The SMART approach described in chapter 4 can and has been applied to balanced scorecard data. In the balanced scorecard context, SMART provides a framework for systematically assessing performance over the four perspectives included in the balanced scorecard approach. The example cases discussed here demonstrate that.

Balanced scorecards have been widely applied in general, and can also consider risk management. Balanced scorecards offer the flexibility to include any type of key measure to planning and operations in any type of organization. They provide a useful means to benchmark and monitor performance and to identify specific areas of weakness.

EPILOGUE

Recapitulation

This book has tried to give a snapshot of risk management as applied to supply chains. It focuses on the key decisions of source selection, but methods demonstrated can be applied to any supply chain selection decision, including facility location, channel selection, and transportation route selection.

The core of the book is that there are modeling tools of various types that can support supply chain management. These include risk matrices for planning, SMART and Monte Carlo simulations for analysis, and balanced scorecards for monitoring organizational performance.

Chapter 1 introduced the many risks and unexpected consequences involved in supply chain management.

Chapter 2 described a generic risk management process as applied to supply chains and elaborated on specific supply chain risks. Various information technology and management control systems that have been applied to retail supply chains were described. Robust strategies were suggested.

Chapter 3 presented risk matrices, a planning tool that has been applied to identify potential supply chain risks.

Chapter 4 focused on the SMART technique to support decision making under multiple criteria conditions. A source selection context was used for demonstration, but again, selection decisions occur in a number of supply chain contexts, including facility location, channel selection, and transportation route selection.

Chapter 5 introduced the Monte Carlo simulation approach to analyze conditions of risk as described by probability distributions. This requires software that is obtainable from various vendors, some of which were identified. Monte Carlo simulation is a powerful and flexible tool appropriate to a number of supply chain problems.

Chapter 6 focused on Monte Carlo simulation applied to vendor selection. The concept of value at risk was discussed in the supply chain management context.

Chapter 7 demonstrated simple linear programming optimization tools important in supply chain management. The basic model introduced was a transportation model, capable of identifying the low-cost assignment of sources to demands. A multiple-objective linear programming model of a simplified aluminum supply chain was then demonstrated. These models were meant to introduce the concept. Detailed modeling of much more complex models is a well-developed field.

Chapter 8 dealt with balanced scorecards, a monitoring technique. This graphical approach has been applied to monitor organizational performance in risk contexts in a number of cases.

Throughout the book, reports of real supply chain risk management applications were provided.

Supply chains offer many opportunities to globalize business, utilizing relative cost advantages worldwide. However, accessing these lower-cost sources introduces a variety of risks and unexpected consequences. Hopefully this short book has provided an introduction for readers to consider opportunities and associated risks in the context of their specific supply chains.

Notes

Chapter 1

1. Nankivell (2004).
2. Coy (2011).
3. Nelson (2010).
4. Uhlmann (2010).
5. Pearson and Read (2010).
6. Einhorn et al. (2011).
7. Reiter and Cremer (2011).
8. Pearson and Read (2010).
9. Cucchiella and Gastaldi (2006).

Chapter 2

1. Ritchie and Brindley (2007a).
2. Mentzer et al. (2001).
3. Tang (2006).
4. Rice and Caniato (2003).
5. Hopkins (2003).
6. Mukherjee (2008).
7. Mitroff and Alpasan (2003).
8. Sterman (1989).
9. Fisher and Raman (1996).
10. Cachon and Fisher (2000); Chen et al. (2001).
11. Holweg et al. (2005).
12. Kaipia et al. (2002).
13. Cohen Kulp (2002).
14. Fry et al. (2001).
15. Kraiselburd et al. (2004).
16. Vergin (1998).
17. Fliedner (2003).
18. Micheau (2005).

19. Lee and Preston (2012).

20. World Economic Forum (2013).

21. Tang (2006).

22. Cook (1998).

23. Fishman (2006).

24. Ritchie and Brindley (2007b).

25. Kleindorfer and Saad (2005).

Chapter 3

1. Blomeyer et al. (2009).

2. McIlwain (2006).

3. Cox (2008).

4. TECHNEAU (2009).

5. Yang (2010).

6. Day (2007).

7. Henselwood and Phillips (2006).

8. Yang (2010).

Chapter 4

1. Olson (1996).

2. Neiger et el. (2009).

3. Edwards (1977).

4. Cucchiella and Gastaldi (2006).

5. Wu and Olson (2010).

6. Rezaei and Ortt (2012).

7. Barker and Zabinsky (2011).

8. Kirkwood et al. (2005).

Chapter 5

1. Evans and Olson (2005).

2. Klibi and Martel (2012).

3. For a more complete description of Monte Carlo simulation, see Evans and Olson (2005).

Chapter 6

1. Hubbard (2009).
2. Markowitz (1952).
3. Olson (1996).
4. Gordon (2009).
5. Jorion (1997).
6. Sawik (2011).
7. Rockafellar and Uryasev (2002).

Chapter 7

1. Brown et al. (1983).
2. Dauzère-Pérès et al. (2007).
3. Onur Mete and Zabinsky (2010).
4. Hillier and Lieberman (2009).

Chapter 8

1. Kaplan and Norton (1992).
2. Fishman (2006).
3. Holzner (2006).
4. Al-Mashari et al. (2003).
5. Kaplan and Norton (2006).
6. Schaefer et al. (2006).
7. Beasley et al. (2006).
8. Campbell et al. (2006).
9. Sugarman and Kakabadse (2008).
10. Janssen et al. (2006).
11. Eom, Yun, and Paek (2008).
12. Duran and Cordova (2012).
13. Varma and Deshmukh (2009).
14. Bhagwat and Sharma (2007).

References

Aabo, T., J.R.S. Fraser, and B.J. Simkins. 2005. "The Rise and Evolution of the Chief Risk Officer: Enterprise Risk Management at Hydro One." *Journal of Applied Corporate Finance* 17, no. 3, pp. 62–75.

Al-Mashari, M., A. Al-Mudimigh, and M. Zairi. 2003. "Enterprise Resource Planning: A Taxonomy of Critical Factors." *European Journal of Operational Research* 146, no. 2, pp. 352–64.

Barker, T.J., and Z.B. Zabinsky. 2011. "A Multicriteria Decision Making Model for Reverse Logistics Using Analytical Hierarchy Process." *Omega* 39, no. 5, pp. 558–73.

Beasley, M., A. Chen, K. Nunez, and L. Wright. 2006. "Working Hand in Hand: Balanced Scorecards and Enterprise Risk Management." *Strategic Finance* 87, no. 9, pp. 49–55.

Bhagwat, R., and M.K. Sharma. 2007. "Performance Measurement of Supply Chain Management Using the Analytical Hierarchy Process." *Production Planning & Control* 18, no. 8, pp. 666–80.

Bhatia, G., C. Lane, and A. Wain. 2013. *Building Resilience in Supply Chains: An Initiative of the Risk Response Network in Collaboration with Accenture*. Geneva: World Economic Forum.

Blomeyer, D., K. Coneus, M. Laucht, and F. Pfeiffer. 2009. "Initial Risk Matrix, Home Resources, Ability Development, and Children's Achievement." *Journal of the European Economic Association* 7, no. 2–3, pp. 638–48.

Brown, M., A. Dammert, A. Meeraus, and A. Stoutjesdijk. 1983. *Worldwide Investment Analysis: The Case of Aluminum*. (World Bank Staff Working Paper 603). Washington: The World Bank.

Cachon, G., and M. Fisher. 2000. "Supply Chain Inventory Management and the Value of Shared Information." *Management Science* 46, no. 8, pp. 1032–48.

Campbell, M., G.W. Adams, D.R. Campbell, and M.R. Rose. 2006. "Internal Audit Can Deliver More Value." *Financial Executive* 22, no. 1, pp. 44–47.

Chen, F., A. Federgruen, and Y.S. Zheng. 2001. "Coordination Mechanisms for a Distribution System with One Supplier and Multiple Retailers." *Management Science* 47, no. 5, pp. 693–708.

Cohen Kulp, S. 2002. "The Effect of Information Precision and Reliability on Manufacturer-Retailer Relationships." *The Accounting Review* 77, no. 3, pp. 653–677.

Cook, T. 1998. "Sabre Soars." *OR/MS Today*, June.

Cox, L.A., Jr. 2008. "What's Wrong with Risk Matrices?" *Risk Analysis* 28, no. 2, pp. 497–512.

Cucchiella, F., and M. Gastaldi. 2006. "Risk Management in Supply Chain: A Real Option Approach." *Journal of Manufacturing Technology Management* 17, no. 6, pp. 700–20.

Day, G.S. 2007. "Is It Real? Can We Win? Is It Worth Doing? Managing Risk and Reward in An Innovation Portfolio." *Harvard Business Review* 85, no. 12, pp. 110–20.

Duran, C., and F. Cordova. 2012. "Conceptual Analysis for the Strategic and Operational Knowledge Management of a Port Community." *Informatica Economica* 16, no. 2, pp. 35–44.

Edwards, W. 1977. "How to Use Multiattribute Utility Measurement for Social Decision Making." *IEEE Transactions on Systems, Man, and Cybernetics, SMC* 7, no. 5, 326–40.

Einhorn, B., T. Culpan, and A. Ohnsman. March, 2011. "Now, a Weak Link the Global Supply Chain." *Bloomberg Businessweek* 4221, pp. 18–19.

Eom, C.S.J., S.H. Yun, and J.H. Paek. 2008. "Subcontractor Evaluation and Management Framework for Strategic Partnering." *Journal of Construction Engineering and Management* 134, no. 11, pp. 842–51.

Evans, J.R., and D.L. Olson. 2005. *Simulation and Risk Analysis.* Englewood Cliffs, NJ: Prentice-Hall.

Fisher, M., and A. Raman. 1996. "Reducing the Cost of Demand Uncertainty through Accurate Response to Early Sales." *Operations Research* 44, no. 1, pp. 87–99.

Fishman, C. 2006. *The Wal-Mart Effect: How the World's Most Powerful Company Really Works – And How It's Transforming the American Economy.* NY: Penguin.

Fliedner, G. 2003. "CPFR: An Emerging Supply Chain Tool." *Industrial Management & Data Systems* 103, no. 1, pp. 14–21.

Fry, M.J., R. Kapuscinski, and T. Lennon Olsen. 2001. "Coordinating Production and Delivery Under a (z, Z)-type Vendor-managed Inventory Contract." *Manufacturing & Service Operations Management* 3, no. 2, pp. 151–73.

Gordon, A.J. 2009. "From Markowitz to Modern Risk Management." *European Journal of Finance* 15, no. 5/6, pp. 451–61.

Henselwood, F., and G. Phillips. 2006. "A Matrix-based Risk Assessment Approach for Addressing Linear Hazards Such as Pipelines." *Journal of Loss Prevention in the Process Industries* 19, no. 5, pp. 433–41.

Hillier, F.S., and G.L. Lieberman. 2010. *Introduction to Operations Research.* 9th ed. New York: McGraw-Hill.

Holzner, S. 2006. *How Dell Does It: Using Speed and Innovation to Achieve Extraordinary Results.* NY: McGraw-Hill.

Holweg, M., S. Disney, J. Holström, and J. Småros. 2005. "Supply Chain Collaboration: Making Sense of the Strategy Continuum." *European Management Journal* 23, no. 2, pp. 170–81.

Hopkins, K. January, 2005. "Value Opportunity Three: Improving the Ability to Fulfill Demand." *Business Week.*

Hubbard, D.W. 2009. *The Failure of Risk Management: Why It's Broken and How to Fix It.* Hoboken, NJ: John Wiley & Sons.

Janssen, A., S.F. Lienin, F. Gassmann, and A. Wokaun. 2006. "Model Aided Policy Development for the Market Penetration of Natural Gas Vehicles in Switzerland." *Transportation Research Part A* 40, pp. 316–33.

Jorion, P. 1997. *Value at Risk: The New Benchmark for Controlling Market Risk.* NY: McGraw-Hill.

Kaipia, R., J. Holmström, and K. Tanskanen. 2002. "VMI: What are You Losing If You Let Your Customer Place Orders?" *Production Planning & Control* 13, no. 1, pp. 17–25.

Kaplan, R.S., and D.P. Norton. 1992. "The Balanced Scorecard – Measures that Drive Performance." *Harvard Business Review* 70, no. 1, pp. 71–79.

Kaplan, R.S., and D.P. Norton. 2006. *Alignment: Using the Balanced Scorecard to Create Corporate Synergies.* Cambridge, MA: Harvard Business School Press Books.

Keeney, R.L. 1992. *Value-Focused Thinking: A Path to Creative Decisionmaking.* Cambridge, MA: Harvard University Press.

Kleindorfer, P.R., and G.H. Saad. 2005. "Managing Disruption Risks in Supply Chains." *Production and Operations Management* 14, no. 1, pp. 53–68.

Klibi, W., and A. Martel. 2012. "Scenario-based Supply Chain Network Risk Modeling." *European Journal of Operational Research* 223, pp. 644–58.

Kraiselburd, S., V.G. Narayanan, and A. Raman. 2004. "Contracting in a Supply Chain with Stochastic Demand and Substitute Products." *Production and Operations Management* 13, no. 1, pp. 46–62.

Lee, B., and F. Preston. 2012. *Preparing for High-impact, Low-probability Events: Lessons from Eyjafjallajökull.* London: A Chatham House Report.

Markowitz, H.M. 1952. "The Utility of Wealth." *Journal of Political Economy* LIX, no. 3, pp. 151–7.

McIlwain, J.C. 2006. "A Review: A Decade of Clinical Risk Management and Risk Tools." *Clinician in Management* 14, no. 4, pp. 189–99.

Mentzer, J.T., W. Dewitt, J.S. Keebler, S. Min, N.W. Nix, C.D. Smith, and Z.G. Zacharia. 2001. *Supply Chain Management.* Thousand Oaks, CA: Sage.

Micheau, V.A. 2005. "How Boeing and Alcoa Implemented a Successful Vendor Managed Inventory Program." *The Journal of Business Forecasting* Spring, pp. 17–19.

Mitroff, I., and M. Alpasan. 2003. "Preparing for Evil." *Harvard Business Review* 81, no. 4, pp. 109–15.

Mukherjee, A.S. 2008. *The Spider's Strategy: Creating Networks to Advert Crisis, Create Change, and Really Get Ahead.* London: FT Press.

Nankivell, K.L. 2004. "Troubled Waters." *Foreign Policy* 145, pp. 30–31.

Neiger, D., K. Rotaru, and L. Churilov. 2009. "Supply Chain Risk Identification with Value-focused Process Engineering." *Journal of Operations Management* 27, pp. 154–68.

Nelson, R. May, 2010. "Flight Disruption Lacks Hard Data." *Test & Measurement World* 30, p. 4.

Olson, D.L. 1996. *Decision Aids for Selection Problems*. New York: Springer.

Onur Mete, H., and Z.B. Zabinsky. 2010. "Stochastic Optimization of Medical Supply Location and Distribution in Disaster Management." *International Journal of Production Economics* 126, pp. 76–84.

Pearson, M., and B. Read. June 2010. "A Volcano's Fallout: Strategies for Disruption." *Businessweek.*

Reiter, C., and A. Cremer. January 2011. "Volkswagen, BMW Feel Pinch from Struggling Suppliers." *Bloomberg Businessweek.*

Rezaei, J., and R. Ortt. 2012. "A Multi-variable Approach to Supplier Segmentation." *International Journal of Production Research* 50, no. 16, pp. 4593–611.

Rice, J.B., Jr., and F. Caniato. 2003. "Supply Chain Response to Terrorism: Creating Resilient and Secure Supply Chains." In *Supply Chain Response to Terrorism Project Interim Report*, ed. J.B. Rice. Cambridge, MA: MIT Center for Transportation and Logistics.

Ritchie, B., and C. Brindley. 2007a. "Supply Chain Risk Management and Performance: A Guiding Framework for Future Development." *International Journal of Operations & Production Management* 27, no. 3, pp. 303–22.

Ritchie, B., and C. Brindley. 2007b. "An Emergent Framework for Supply Chain Risk Management and Performance Measurement." *Journal of the Operational Research Society* 58, no. 11, pp. 1398–411.

Rockafellar, R.T., and S. Uryassev. 2002. "Conditional Value-at-risk for General Loss Distributions." *Journal of Banking & Finance* 26, no. 7, pp. 1443–71.

Sawik, T. 2011. "Supplier Selection in Make-to-order Environment with Risks." *Mathematical and Computer Modelling* 53, pp. 1670–9.

Schaefer, A., M. Cassidy, K. Marshall, and J. Rossi. 2006. "Internal Audits and Executive Education: A Holy Alliance to Reduce Theft and Misreporting." *Employee Relations Law Journal* 32, no. 1, pp. 61–84.

Sterman, J.D. 1989. "Modeling Managerial Behavior: Misperceptions of Feedback in a Dynamic Decision Making Experiment." *Management Science* 35, pp. 321–39.

Sugarman, P., and N. Kakabadse. 2008. "A Model of Mental Health Governance." *The International Journal of Clinical Leadership* 16, pp. 17–26.

Tang, C.S. 2006. "Robust Strategies for Mitigating Supply Chain Disruptions." *International Journal of Logistics: Research and Applications* 9, no. 1, pp. 33–45.

Törnqvist, M., B. öfverström, and C. Swartz. 2009. *Risk Assessment Case Study: Upper Mnyameni, South Africa.* Nieuwegein, the Netherlands: TECHNEAU.

Uhlmann, U. 2010. "Eruption Disruption." *Canadian Underwriter* 77, no. 8, pp. 18–20.

Vergin, R.C. 1998. "An Examination of Inventory Turnover in the Fortune 500 Industrial Companies." *Production and Inventory Management Journal* 39, pp. 51–56.

Wu, D.D., and D.L. Olson. 2010. "Enterprise Risk Management: A DEA VaR Approach in Vendor Selection." *International Journal of Production Research* 48, no. 16, pp. 4919–32.

Index

Accounting risk, 49
Adjustable cells, 93
Advanced planning system costs, 65.
    See also Net Present Value
    (NPV)
Alliances, 26
Asset impairment risk, 49

Backorder, 68
Balanced scorecards, 118–120, 124
    applied to subcontractors, 116–118
    definition of, 111
    ERM and, 113–116
    global outsourcing, perspectives of,
        122
    perspectives of, 111
    petroleum supply chain, 120–121
    purpose of, 122
    values, 123
Bird flu, 3
Bounded/boundedness solution,
    98–99
Bullwhip effect, 17
Bullwhip phenomenon, 19
Business
    modern way of conducting, 11
    organizations, 6, 8
    uncertainty in, 14

Canadian forces medical supply
    system, 108–109
Carrying costs, 68
Changing cells, 93. *See also* Adjustable
    cells
Channel selection, 109
Cognitive psychology, 43
    research into, 13
Collaboration, 12
Collaborative planning, forecasting,
    and replenishment (CPFR),
    21–22

Commercial carpet recycling value
    calculation, 57
Commoditization of products and
    services, 11
Competition, 5
Competitive risk, 49
Continuous replenishment (CR),
    21. *See also* vendor-managed
    inventory (VMI)
Conventional solution process,
    44
Coordination, 12
Cost trade-off, 11
Credit risks, 30
Cross-organizational supply chains,
    11
Crystal Ball basic inventory model,
    71, 73
Crystal Ball simulation software,
    61, 64, 66–67, 76
Customer perspective, 112
Customer risk, 49

Decision makers, 44
Decision support system (DSS),
    58, 106–107. *See also* IBM
    decision support system
Degeneracy, 99
Dell, 1, 111
Demand management, 17–18
Deployment, 63
Disaster management, information
    flow in, 108
Disruption risks, 13
Downside risk, 49
Drake, Francis, 3
Dual prices, 99
Dynamic assortment planning,
    26
Dynamic pricing and promotion,
    25–26

E-business, 18
Economic supply incentives, 25
Electronic data interchange (EDI), 20
Enterprise resource planning (ERP)
    system, 22
Enterprise risk, 113
Enterprise risk management
    framework, 30
E-procurement, 14
Excel, 58, 61, 66, 88, 93, 100, 107
Excess inventory, 21

Feasibility solution, 98–99
Financial perspective, 111
Financial risk, 49
Flexible supply base, 24
Flexible transportation, 25
Frontline Solver, 61, 76, 81, 88
Functions, 91

Globalization, 2–5
Global operations, 58

Hanseatic League, 2
Hardware, 64–65
Hedging activities, 34
Hierarchy structuring, 43–46
Holding costs, 68. *See also* carrying
    costs

IBM decision support system,
    57–60
Infeasible solution, 99
Information management,
    18–19
Information system coordination, 17
Information technology (IT), 19
Innovation, 113
Integer models, 99–100
Internal business operations, 113
Internal controls, 34
Internal risk management, 8
Internet, 20
Inventory model solution, 102
Inventory simulation model,
    69–70

Inventory system
    costs, components of, 68–69
    decisions, 68
    definition of, 67
    formulas for, 70
    risks associated with, 68

Just-in-time delivery, 14

Land supply chains, 12
Lean manufacturing system,
    5, 13, 67–68
Learning, 113
Legal risks, 30, 49
Linear programming (LP) models,
    109–110, 126
    applying to supply chains, 90
    assumptions
        certainty, 97
        continuity, 97–98
        linearity, 95–97
    complications, 98–99
    components of, 90–91
    demonstration model, 91–93
    generate solutions for objective
        function, 109
    in operation management, 89
    solutions to optimize problems,
        93–95
    transportation, 94
Lost sale, 69

Make-and-buy strategy, 24–25
Market risks, 30
Means objectives, 44
Medical device recycling value
    calculation, 56
Military organizations, 1
Mixed-integer optimization of
    transportation plans, 108–109
Monte Carlo simulation, 8, 61–62,
    66, 75–76, 79, 88, 121,
    125–126
Multiple attribute utility theory
    (MAUT), 47
Multiple optimal solution, 98–99

National Health Service Litigation
   Authority, 31
Natural disasters, 22–23
Natural risks, 6
Net Present Value (NPV), 64–67
Nobel, Alfred, 6
Northridge earthquake, 3–4

Operation/operational risks,
   13, 17, 30
Ordering costs, 68
Outsourcing, 5
   impact, supply chain risks
      assessed for, 49
   increases external uncertainties, 48
   measurement of internal business
      operations of, 113
   organizations, 77
   vendors, 113

Packaged aspirin, 2
Piracy, 3
Pirate attacks, 3
Postponement, 24
Product management, 18
Product risk, 49
Purchasing costs, 69

Quantity discount, 69
Queen Elizabeth I, 3

Radio frequency identification
   (RFID), 16, 18, 27
Redeployment, 63
Reduced costs, 99
Regulatory risk, 49
Reorder point (ROP), 69–70, 72–75
Reputation risk, 49
Residential carpet recycling value
   calculation, 56
Retailer-managed inventory, 20
Retailers, 19, 21
Risk, 12
   analysis, 34
   appetite, 29
   assessment, 13–14

avoidance, 14–15
evaluation, 34
exposure within supply chains, 26–27
identification, 13, 29
mitigation, 15
ranking, calculation of scenario, 37
ratings, 34
reduction/control, 34
review, 29
Risk management process, 29
   alternative outcomes, 40–41
   definition of, 77
   key to successful, 77
   in supply chains, 12–15
Risk matrix/matrices, 29
   application of, 38–41
   characteristics of, 34
   for consequence and frequency, 38
   dimensions of, 39
   for Federal Highway
      Administration, 33
   for health consequences, 36–37
   health effects, 35–36
   idea of color-coded, 42
   of medical events, 31–33
   for people affected, 36–37
   product, 31
   reveal distribution of risk, 34
Route selection, 109

Security per ship, increased annual
   costs of, 3
Severe acute respiratory syndrome
   (SARS), 3, 22
Shared risk, 49
Shipping decision, 106–107
Shortage/stock-out costs, 68–69
Sichuan earthquake, 4
Silent product rollover, 26
Silk Road, 2
Simple multiattribute rating theory
   (SMART), 45
Simulations, 61
   Crystal Ball simulation software
      (see Crystal Ball simulation
      software)

distributions and probabilities used, 79

features of, 74–75

Monte Carlo simulation (*see* Monte Carlo simulation)

results, 81

supply chain risk simulation (*see* supply chain risk simulation)

SMART technique, 8, 47–48, 54–55, 60, 121, 124–125

Software, 43, 64–65, 72, 75, 88, 125

Strategic risk, 30

Strategic stock, 24

Supplier (vendor) evaluation, 17

Supplier management process
  product design selection, 54–57
  steps in, 52
  supplier segmentation criteria by category, 53

Supplier risk, 49

Supplier segmentation criteria by category, 53

Supplier segmentation management, concept of, 53

Supplier segmentation process, 52

Supply chain coordination systems
  collaborative planning, forecasting, and replenishment (CPFR) (*see* collaborative planning, forecasting, and replenishment (CPFR))
  continuous replenishment (CR) (*see* continuous replenishment (CR))
  efficient customer response, 19–20
  vendor-managed inventory (VMI) (*see* vendor-managed inventory (VMI))

Supply chain demonstration model, 101–106

Supply chain management decisions, 43
  hierarchy structuring (*see* hierarchy structuring)
  source selection, 48–52
  value hierarchy (*see* value hierarchy)

Supply chain network hazard modeling, 62–64

Supply chain optimization model, 106–107

Supply chain outsourcing, 48

Supply chain risk management, 12, 34–38

Supply chain risk model, 77–83

Supply chain risk simulation, 62–64

Supply chains, 2, 5, 26, 126
  alliances, 14
  benefits of, 1
  complex system of networks, 12
  connected sources of goods to customers, 1
  core organizations, 8
  decisions, 11
  disruptions in 2012, 23
  internal and external risk, 6–7
  involves inventories between elements, 67
  linear programming models applying to, 90
  resilience, 22–23
  robust strategies to cope with disruption, 24–26

Supply chain simulation, 86–87

Supply chains risk, 2–5, 14, 61
  categories of
    demand management (*see* demand management)
    information management (*see* information management)
    product management (*see* product management)
    supply management (*see* supply management)

Supply
  disruption, 49
  management, 15–17

Sustainment, 63

Swing weighting/weights, 54–55, 58, 123
  development of, 50

Taiwanese shipping risk matrix, 40

Target cell, 93

TECHNEAU project, 34

Toyota, 1

Trade in Baltic and North Seas, 2

Unbounded solution, 98–99
Uncertainty, 61
Unexpected consequences, 5–8
Unfortunate events, 77
Unique optimal solution, 98–99

Value at risk (VaR) concept, 83
    and vendor selection, 84–85
Value-focused approach, 44
Value hierarchy, 43–45
    for supply chain risk, 46
Value judgments, 44

Value score calculation, 52
Variables, 91
Vendor alternative scores, 51
Vendor-managed inventory (VMI),
    20–22
Vendor selection simulation model,
    80, 84–85

Walmart, 1, 17–18, 111
Water system, 35

Zero-one programming, 100–101

OTHER TITLES IN OUR SUPPLY AND OPERATIONS MANAGEMENT COLLECTION

Johnny Rungtusanatham, The Ohio State University, Editor

- *Global Supply Chain Management* by Matt Drake
- *Managing Commodity Price Risk: A Supply Chain Perspective* by George A. Zsidisin
- *Improving Business Performance With Lean* by James Bradley
- *RFID for the Supply Chain and Operations Professional* by Pamela Zelbst
- *Insightful Quality: Beyond Continuous Improvement* by Victor Sower
- *Sustainability Delivered Designing Socially and Environmentally Responsible Supply Chains* by Madeleine Pullman
- *Strategic Leadership of Portfolio and Project Management* by Timothy J. Kloppenborg
- *Sustainable Operations and Closed-Loop Supply Chains* by Gilvan Souza
- *Mapping Workflows and Managing Knowledge Capturing Formal and Tacit Knowledge to Improve Performance* by John Kmetz
- *Supply Chain Planning: Practical Frameworks for Superior Performance* by Matthew Liberatore
- *Understanding the Dynamics of the Value Chain* by William Presutti
- *An Introduction to Supply Chain Management: A Global Supply Chain Support Perspective* by Edmund Prater
- *Project Strategy and Strategic Portfolio Management: A Primer* by William H. A. Johnson
- *Sourcing to Support the Green Initiative* by Lisa Ellram
- *Designing Supply Chains for New Product Development* by Antonio Arreola-Risa
- *The Management and Improvement of Business Processes: Approaches, Models, Techniques* by Kaushik Sengupta
- *Project Management Made Easy: A Practical Guide for Executives and Professionals* by Nand Dhameja
- *Metric Dashboards for Operations and Supply Chain Excellence* by Jaideep Motwani and Rob Ptacek
- *Statistical Process Control for Managers* by Victor E. Sower

Announcing the Business Expert Press Digital Library

*Concise E-books Business Students Need
for Classroom and Research*

This book can also be purchased in an e-book collection by your library as

- a one-time purchase,
- that is owned forever,
- allows for simultaneous readers,
- has no restrictions on printing, and
- can be downloaded as PDFs from within the library community.

Our digital library collections are a great solution to beat the rising cost of textbooks. E-books can be loaded into their course management systems or onto students' e-book readers.

The **Business Expert Press** digital libraries are very affordable, with no obligation to buy in future years. For more information, please visit **www.businessexpertpress.com/librarians**. To set up a trial in the United States, please email **sales@businessexpertpress.com**.

CPSIA information can be obtained at www.ICGtesting.com
Printed in the USA
BVOW03s1540100914

366013BV00005B/20/P

9 781631 570575